Media Training 101

A Guide to Meeting the Press

SALLY STEWART

WILEY

John Wiley & Sons, Inc.

To my mentor, teacher, and friend,
Linda Levinson,
with deepest gratitude and respect.

For general information on our other products and services, or technical support, please contact our Customer Care Department within the United States at 800-762-2974, outside the United States at 317-572-3993 or fax 317-572-4002.

Wiley also publishes its books in a variety of electronic formats. Some content that appears in print may not be available in electronic books. For more information about Wiley products, visit our web site at www.wiley.com.

ISBN 0-471-27155-1

Printed in the United States of America.

10 9 8 7 6 5 4 3 2

CONTENTS

PREFACE

In just a few minutes, when you finish reading this Preface and turn to Chapter 1, you will be launching an initiative to prepare you to seek out reporters and publicize your company's achievements. Before you begin learning the principles of *Media Training 101*, such as the Foundational Rules for Media Success, the Organic Keyword Method, and the ABC Template for Answering Any Question, I want to ask you as I ask all my clients at our first meeting: Do you have a firm commitment to building a quality public relations (PR) program?

If you do, then what I am about to say will not scare you away. I don't want you to get too comfortable, though. Especially these days, a little bit of fear is healthy when you start dealing with reporters.

That is because journalists are angry. Irritated. Irate. Annoyed. Infuriated. Outraged. Furious. Oh heck, they are just plain pissed off.

Why? Because people lied to them.

Throughout the entire dot-com build up and bust, company leaders told reporters that the future of business was in a company's potential. Don't look at the bottom line, business people said. Look instead at my company's potential to have a bigger bottom line down the road.

Journalists not only bought that reasoning, they championed it. They wrote story after story heralding start-up companies that were going to change the world by selling dog food over the Internet or buying up excess energy. They invited CEOs on their television programs when the CEOs' companies never made a profit. Some of them never even made it out of the development phase to make a product.

What became of all that coverage? When the dot-com bubble burst a couple of years ago, journalists wiped the egg off their faces and began covering the remains of the story: Pets.com, Enron, HealthSouth, and Martha Stewart. Now, they are still covering those stories, but they are covering them with a more critical eye, asking tougher questions and demanding proof.

There are few things in the world that irk reporters (and their editors and producers) more than plain flat out missing the story. There they were, publishing and airing huge, flattering stories about various companies' *potential* and all the while, it now seems, some of those very companies were cooking the books, defrauding state energy buyers, and stealing the money out of their investors' retirement plans.

So now, a few years later, here you come, having built a company or created a new and improved widget, and you are looking for coverage. Well, brace yourself, because if you thought journalists were tough before, just try pulling one over on them now.

In other words, be afraid. Be very afraid.

As we will see in the chapters ahead, journalists are not your friends. They might behave as though they are your friends, and in the heat of an interview, they really mean it. Still, the minute a reporter leaves the scene of an interview, the only loyalty they have is not to friendship, but to the story. If covering the story means that a reporter nods sympathetically during an interview and then uses the same facts his sympathetic nods helped elicit to cast doubts on your business, then they will do it.

For proof, all you have to do is open to the first page of *The Journalist and The Murderer* by Janet Malcomb (Random House, 1990), an esteemed journalist herself. More than a decade ago, Malcomb wrote:

> Every journalist who is not too stupid or too full of himself to notice what is going on knows that what he does is morally indefensible. He is a kind of confidence man, preying on people's vanity, ignorance, or loneliness, gaining their trust and betraying them without remorse. Like the credulous widow who wakes up one day to find the charming young man and all

her savings gone, so the consenting subject of a piece of non-fiction writing learns—when the article or book appears—his hard lesson. Journalists justify their treachery in various ways according to their temperaments. The more pompous talk about freedom of speech and "the public's right to know"; the least talented talk about Art; the seemliest murmur about earning a living.

I first read Malcomb's words when I was a reporter myself—and they rang so true that they stung. Even then, it seemed unfair. Reporters and producers have all this power because thousands, even millions, believe what they read in the newspaper, what they hear on the radio and what they see on television. It doesn't matter if a reporter makes a mistake or even if the mistake is corrected the next day. The initial story has already made an impact that cannot be erased.

In comparison, the person being interviewed—even the mighty, the powerful and the wealthy—have little power. If they protest the story, they look like wimps. If they fight back, they risk attracting more scrutiny from more journalists.

Doesn't seem fair that any one group has that much power, does it?

Well, they don't anymore—as long as you keep reading this book. And reading it. And reading it.

Use *Media Training 101* as a guidebook into the locker room mentality of journalists. Find out what makes them tick. Scribble in the margins and dog-ear the pages. Make *Media Training 101* work for you.

If there is one lesson I want you to remember from this book, it is that when you deal with the media, you need to first take a deep breath and then show a little *chutzpah*, which is a Yiddish word that, in its best use, means to demonstrate a little bit of heart and a lot of moxie. Don't just get lulled into submission by a reporter who acts like your good buddy. Stay in control of your own message by knowing what you want to say and what you don't.

For years, big, wealthy companies have been able to exert some measure of control over stories about their businesses because of one simple fact: *These companies can afford media training.*

It isn't cheap to hire a qualified media trainer. For just a half-day session, a decent media trainer charges anywhere from $5,000 to $20,000. Someone with a budding business can't afford that. But they can afford the cost of this book to find out what journalists don't want you to know.

Some of my best friends are journalists, so I don't say this lightly: Journalists want to keep all the control and power on their side of the interview equation. It makes their job easier to have a less sophisticated story subject.

After all, someone who has never been media trained doesn't know how to define their own story, make sure that "off the record" really does mean "off the record," or how to turn down a reporter's request without turning off future media opportunities.

There are few things in business more dangerous than a successful public relations program, for once you invite reporters to take a peek inside your company and publish or broadcast their findings, you are also inviting their scrutiny. If you do not possess a firm commitment to handling your company's PR program with care, then you will not be able to control the coverage your company receives. A lack of control is fine as long as the coverage is positive, but as a former reporter for USA Today, I can tell you that reporters are always looking for new stories and new angles. If you don't pay attention to your company's public image and PR program, you might not like some of the coverage your company gets.

Before he ever met me, one client of mine was involved in a contentious business deal with a major professional sports governing body. A reporter got wind of the deal and called the client to ask about it. The client said that he'd talk, but only off the record. The reporter said sure. The client spilled everything, including his unflattering opinions on the major business people involved in the deal. The next day, the reporter published a front-page story that included everything my client said, attributed to him. As a consequence, the sports business backed out of the deal and my client lost hundreds of thousands of dollars.

The client called the reporter and said, "How could you do this when our conversation was off the record?"

The reporter said, "I don't believe in off the record."

We could debate that reporter's ethics for days. It won't change the fact that the story got into print and cost the client dearly.

So how do you prevent such a horror story from happening to you?

As a result of consulting with hundreds of major companies and helping them to attain positive news coverage, I know that the companies with the most successful public relations programs have three traits in common:

1. They invest resources, including time and attention, into public relations.
2. They rely on facts to spread their message.
3. They see their company's mission as more than just making money.

The Three Commitments for Public Relations Success

I call these characteristics the *Three Commitments*. We review each commitment in detail in this book, and I explain how you and your company can build the Three Commitments into a sturdy foundation for public relations success.

1. *Investment:* Money is not the essential ingredient in the Investment Commitment; *time* is. Your company will not reap media opportunities unless you invest time into developing each step of the public relations process. It takes time to read several reporters' work before you select the one you think might be interested in

writing your story. It takes time to think about and prepare for the kinds of tough questions you can expect a reporter to ask. You need to commit time to talking with reporters and doing interviews.

If you hire a consultant to manage your company's public relations program, you will still need to devote some time to getting the job done right. Even the best consultant cannot know your company as well as you do. A consultant might have good ideas but he or she still needs your input. If an executive doesn't invest time in a public relations program, the results will be mixed at best.

2. *Clear Vision:* Companies that succeed in the public relations arena generally display a commitment to seeing their company's pluses and minuses clearly and without "spin." Although spin has become a popular term for describing the way some public figures communicate with the media, the companies with the most successful PR programs rely on communicating facts without appearing to engage in spin, which connotes using hyperbole and innuendo. Develop your commitment to Clear Vision by resolving to take a tough look at your company. Is the story you are pitching to reporters based on facts? Will reporters ask questions you don't want to or legally cannot answer? What are the good and bad points about your company?

3. *Mission:* Often, I call this commitment "Wearing the White Hat," just like the good guys always do in comic books. The concept is that companies with successful public relations programs present themselves to journalists as being about more than making a profit. They must have a mission that makes it clear that they are the "good guys." For example, a telecommunications company might present its mission as providing small companies with affordable data and voice services so that small companies aren't penalized for their size by paying more than big companies. Another example could be a law firm that specializes in a certain kind of case because the firm's principals believe the outcomes of those cases are important to the justice system. You must be able

to communicate a mission because you will need to explain why your company's story is of interest to a journalist's audience.

Once you pledge to make the Three Commitments, you are ready to learn what *Media Training 101* can achieve for your company. Good luck and remember to visit www.mediatraining101.com to share your success stories.

SALLY STEWART

INTRODUCTION

I decided to write *Media Training 101* for one simple reason: I can't be everywhere at once.

But the media, well, that's a different story. In our information-saturated society, the media is found everywhere you find business. Executives and entrepreneurs who want to succeed in business know that a key ingredient of their success is being comfortable dealing with the media on a regular basis.

It takes much more than a good media image to build a successful business. It takes a good—even a great—idea and the vision and know-how to put that idea into action. It takes solid management, a team of dedicated employees, satisfied customers, the ability to analyze financial data, and the courage to adjust your business plan in response to the constantly changing economic outlook and data. Once you have those basics nailed down, though, there is simply no getting around the fact that in this Information Age of 24-hour business cable television shows and instant business news e-mail updates, any successful business person needs to know how to effectively communicate. Effective communication means that you and your company can influence—even determine—your company's own reputation. No communication means that you are leaving it to outsiders to set the tone of your company's media coverage. If you allow that, then you are allowing someone else to determine your company's image and reputation among customers, employees, strategic partners, and investors. That is way too much power to put into someone else's hands.

Some of my clients have MBA degrees from Harvard and Wharton. Others are the perfect example of the classic American self-taught rags-to-riches entrepreneur. No matter what their background, they all knew all about business. They knew how to interpret a profit-and-loss statement, how to handle employee disputes, and when and how to seek outside financing. Whether they learned it in business school or on-the-job, they learned their lessons well. Handling those complex problems is second nature to them. My clients became prosperous as their companies grew and they thought they knew everything they needed to know to build a successful company.

That is, until the media came calling.

All it takes is one negative story to bring home the power of the media. Companies are terrific at training people to run the business. But who trains an executive how to harness the power of the media to help a company achieve its goals? Just because you can write a business plan or sell a product doesn't mean that you know the best way to explain it in a sound bite. If you have ever been "bitten" by the media, you know how much it can hurt your business.

I know something about that kind of bite. My career has spanned every aspect of mass communications. I have been inside the media and I have been on the sidelines, in front of the camera as well as behind it. I have been a reporter, editor, columnist, and television commentator. I have produced segments for television shows and interviewed newsmakers on the radio. I have been an officer of a high-tech company during the media blitz that accompanied the Internet boom and subsequent bust. As a consultant at large public relations firms, I have handled communications projects for hundreds of companies. All my experience has convinced me that knowing how to communicate about your business is as important as running it.

I began learning the need for effective business communications when I became a journalist. From the moment I walked into the offices of *The Independent Florida Alligator* at the University of

Florida, I began thinking like a reporter. I believed the people, my readers, had a right to know anything they wanted to know and, on their behalf, I would be fearless in asking the tough questions. The tougher the question, the more the person I was interviewing squirmed. The more they squirmed or evaded the question, the more I was certain I was on to something.

Some of my mind-set at the time can be attributed to overzealous college journalism in the late-1970s, when Bob Woodward and Carl Bernstein were heroes to many—especially idealistic college students—for exposing a president who tried to cover up the Watergate scandal and crimes. But it is also true that I reflected the essence of the unique way that a reporter looks at the world: Reporters are on the side of *Truth* and *Freedom of Information* and nothing will get in the way of their pursuit of the story.

Throughout my journalism career, which included 13 years at *USA Today*, I covered some of the most significant news events of our time, from the World Series celebrations to the Los Angeles riots and the O. J. Simpson murder trial. I continued asking the tough questions. I learned how to elicit the facts of the stories I covered by figuring out how to track down even the most elusive sources. I learned how to put the facts together and how to write the facts in a sequence that would make people want to read them. I went into journalism in no small measure because of my desire and intent to help people by giving them the truth behind every story.

After I covered the O. J. Simpson murder trial, it became apparent to me that journalism had changed. Truth was no longer as important as spectacle.

I still wanted to help people. So I decided that I needed to find another way and I went to work at a nonprofit organization. On my first day of work as the director of communications of Public Counsel Law Center, one of the nation's largest pro bono public interest law firm, I realized I didn't know anything about public relations. But I did know a thing or two about being a reporter and maybe I could leverage that knowledge into securing positive coverage for the important issues that Public Counsel dealt with.

The problem, as I saw it, was that reporters were skeptical of public relations people. The rivalry between reporters and public relations pros is as old as public relations itself. Reporters called them "flacks" which is basically a combination of "flattery" and "hack" and not exactly a compliment. Reporters resented that public relations people were paid more than reporters when reporters thought all public relations people did was shill for a living and say whatever would make their client look good, regardless of the underlying truth. Reporters wanted the facts. Public relations people, they thought, were just looking for a free ad. How could I combat that built-in prejudice and get reporters to listen to my side of the story? Public Counsel was involved in some controversial issues, from interracial adoptions and advocacy for the homeless to immigrants' rights. How could I combat reporters' built-in prejudice and get them to listen to our side of the story? How could I interest reporters in covering something that accurately—and, coincidentally, positively—reflected the work we were doing?

Maybe I could take what I knew about covering the news and learn how to communicate Public Counsel's mission to reporters, who would then communicate our story to their audiences. Perhaps if I invented my own techniques that de-emphasized spin and underscored the use of facts, I could communicate through the media but still not allow the media to do my communication for me.

It worked.

In fact, it worked so well that within weeks, Public Counsel was featured in *The New York Times* and members of Public Counsel's Board of Directors—comprised mainly of Southern California's top business executives and lawyers—were coming to me for advice on their cases and their companies. When I started, I didn't know anything about the automotive industry, the high-tech market, the grocery business, or intellectual property protection, but I did know how to teach those executives how to communicate with the media. I began developing some of the principles you will learn in *Media Training 101*, like the Organic Keyword Method and the things you should never say to a reporter. While I taught these executives and lawyers media training, they taught me business.

I learned even more when I left Public Counsel to work for Mike Sitrick at Sitrick And Company. Mike is regarded as one of the nation's pre-eminent experts in managing public relations crises. From Mike, I learned how to steer a company in crisis through media coverage and interviews that could determine whether the company would fold or continue. I learned how to apply my reporting skills to a wider variety of industries and how to get a company's story out while following the disclosure laws for public companies.

By then, it was the late-1990s and the world was in the midst of an unprecedented tech boom, which fueled an unprecedented bull market. You can take the reporter out of journalism, but you can't take the thirst for a good story out of the reporter. Like any reporter, I wanted to be in the middle of that story, the biggest business story of our time. So when I was offered the opportunity to join the senior management team at a high-tech company, I accepted.

We had a great story to tell and great coverage to show for it. Our only problem was timing. The market sank, the tech boom busted, and the recession began to set in. So I went back to agency life.

As a vice president for two international public relations firms, Edelman Public Relations Worldwide and APCO Worldwide, my clients included three of the top 10 on the Fortune 500 list of largest companies and many more companies with household brand names. I brought my basic media training principles to those companies and watched with pride as executives learned how to leverage any media opportunity into a chance to build their company's reputation and brand.

"I used to think this would be the easy part," one CEO of a national retail chain told me. "I used to think it wasn't brain surgery, but you know what? It is. You are constructing what people think about your company. Why didn't they teach me this in business school?"

I heard the same observation too many times to count. Finally, as I wrote my own business plan and started by own consulting group, SA Stewart Communications, I realized I could write this book to share what I know from my lifetime in the media trenches.

Media Training 101 is not a replacement for having a good, knowledgeable public relations consultant on board, but by employing the techniques and principles of *Media Training 101* you will learn how to choose a consultant wisely and how to use their advice to your company's best advantage.

We'll start off in Chapter 1 by learning the Foundational Rules for Media Success. This is where you learn how to work with the media. The most important concept is to recognize that spin is out. The media is wise to executives who undergo media training and come out not answering any questions and sounding too much like a politician. You do need to know what reporters want and you must be truthful and credible when you give it to them. If a reporter thinks you are "spinning"—spewing propaganda instead of calmly listing the facts—they'll brand you as slick and untrustworthy.

You'll learn to avoid the lethal mistakes that can doom any company in an interview, including when to say "no comment." (Short answer: Never.) You will write your company's Key Message Points and learn how to employ them to answer anything—even the sample questions in Chapter 9.

You'll find out how to recognize different reporters' interview styles and how to use that knowledge to play the interview game to your advantage. You will analyze how to dress for an interview and whether your body language adds to or detracts from your credibility.

When the media just shows up, you'll be able to handle the situation. You will be able to put together everything you have learned so that your press releases get the right kind of media attention. You will learn how to create simple press kits that don't end up in the newsroom garbage pail and you will learn how to interest reporters in doing stories about your company.

You will learn how to build and maintain a media profile that appears to be effortless, spontaneous, and natural.

Often, my advice goes against the advice many public relations professionals have been giving for years. For example, many media training coaches teach that you should never answer a direct question but instead, launch into a rehearsed talking point. I tell you to do it differently. The methods in *Media Training 101* will make you more effective and your message more credible to reporters and the general public.

This is a direct effect of our Information Age. More news and information is available at an instant to anyone who searches for it. When you talk to the media, you are really talking to many different audiences through the media. The public can spot a phony in an instant. You don't want to be one of them.

At the end of each chapter, I have assigned *homework*—exercises designed to help you think like a reporter when they cover your story. I encourage you to take the time to thoroughly explore each homework assignment so that you can develop a journalistic mindset and figure out how reporters—and through a reporter's coverage, the public at large—will interpret your company's moves and news.

When you complete *Media Training 101*, you'll be able to get inside a reporter's head just as reporters think they can get inside yours. You will have a clear idea of what to expect when the media shows up and a clearer sense of how to attract media attention when it would benefit your company.

It is my hope that you will find *Media Training 101* helpful to your business and that you will be able to control your message as well as you control your balance sheet.

PART ONE

UNDERSTANDING THE MEDIA

Foundational Rules for Media Success

Lesson Plan

In this chapter, we cover the basics of working with reporters, including the six steps for generating good public relations (PR), explain what reporters want from you and how to deliver on their expectations, and discuss the importance of being realistic about your company's weaknesses—before a reporter uncovers them.

You have built a successful business. Your earnings exceed expectations. You've got all the right employees in all the right places. You're planning to expand, perhaps by acquiring a competitor or opening an operation in Asia.

Congratulations. But, have you given any thought to exactly how you are going to share your dreams with the rest of the business world? After all, sharing your vision is the first step in securing the support you will need to grow your business, attract new customers, and create the excitement your company needs to turn your vision into reality.

As a former reporter who spent 13 years covering major news events for *USA Today* and as a public relations consultant who has worked for some of the most respected and successful companies in the world, I can attest to the power of good media communications. A story about a company can generate orders and trigger investor interest, but if the story is unflattering, it can quash investor enthusiasm and employee morale as well as slash company growth. When a financial analyst receives a call from a reporter about a certain stock, his answers and the resulting story could have great impact on the company. How can you make sure that your company's story is one that will fuel your business goals?

In this book, I give you an insider's view into how reporters and PR operate. I also show you how to present accurate information about your company, its products, and strategies to the press. The media can then deliver the best possible message to an audience comprised of your current and potential customers, employees, business partners, investors, and vendors.

Many of my clients approach me to represent them anywhere from six months to a year before their target date for unveiling a new product, commencing an acquisition, or going public with a significant company development. These clients know about the benefits that media exposure can bring to their businesses. The right stories can attract strategic partners and bigger clients; the right stories can educate the Wall Street community about a company's business model and smooth the path toward securing investments crucial to a company's growth. Positive press also can help to attract and retain top-notch employees, and it can give your company the kind of brand-building image you can't buy, even with the world's largest advertising budget. A flattering magazine profile of a CEO that appears right before his company makes a bid to acquire another company can help ease the negotiations. After reading the profile, the leaders of the soon-to-be-acquired company may feel more comfortable with the CEO.

Unfortunately, bad press can sink a business. The wrong story at the wrong time can rob your company of its future. For example, Martha Stewart Living Omnimedia was hardly the only company exposed in the financial scandals of this new century. However, the unflattering media stories about CEO Martha Stewart that emphasized her arrogance, snobbishness, and disdainful treatment of her colleagues helped fuel government investigations and the drastic slide in the price of the company's stock.

Recklessly plunging into a public relations program without strategic planning can turn clients, vendors, and partners away from doing business with you. Once a negative story is written, it's not easily forgotten.

Before we get started on your media training, let's review a few ground rules that are essential to any successful public relations program. I'll explain these rules in further detail in the coming chapters, but for now, these foundational rules will give you a sense of how journalists approach their job (and your company's story) and what you should do to prepare yourself for generating great publicity:

- Understand how public relations really works.
- Know what reporters really want.
- Not all stories are created equal.
- Measure your pain threshold.
- The Alpha Dog Story leads the pack.
- Beggars are never happy.
- Reporters are not your friends.
- *The New York Times* equals *The Santa Monica Daily Press.*
- Phony is baloney.
- You can't pitch what you don't know.

Understand How Public Relations Really Works

Public perceptions are built over time and so is public demand for a product. I once worked for a CEO who believed—no matter how energetically I argued with him—that a single story would make the phones ring in his order department. Every time we got a story about his company's products into the press, he ordered extra phone lines installed and if they weren't lighting up with consumers placing orders, he was disappointed. Any positive story will make a few consumers open their wallets, but generally, there won't be a tidal wave until the stories build into a pipeline filled with demand, and that takes time and more than one story.

Another one of my clients, Scott Painter, the founder of CarsDirect.com, has the right idea. Scott believes public relations fuels sales, but he knows that there are many steps in the process of getting sales and that just one misstep can undo all of the work that went into getting the story. Here is his step-by-step program.

Seven Steps for Turning PR into Sales

Step 1   *Awareness:* A consumer reads a story and becomes aware that the product and/or company exists. This step is particularly important in the development of new companies that don't have a lengthy history or a strong consumer following.

Step 2   *Interest:* A consumer reads another story and, as a result, becomes interested in learning more. Alternatively, the consumer hears about the story from someone who read it firsthand. His interest has begun to grow and he now wants to know more about the product and your company.

Step 3   *Action:* Another story might prompt the consumer to ask a friend about the product or to do some research about it on the Internet, or perhaps the story generates interest from another reporter at another publication. (Reporters read other publications to look for story ideas.)

Step 4   *Understanding:* The consumer reads another story or studies his Internet research to begin to understand how the product might help his life or business.

Step 5   *Advocating:* As the company's publicity continues to grow, the consumer reads yet another story and begins to discuss with colleagues, friends, and family members his intent to buy the product.

Step 6   *Buying:* The next story prompts the consumer to purchase the product. At this step, the consumer has high expectations for the product. He anticipates that his experience with the product will match the flattering stories he has read. (Indeed, although the media is often criticized for being biased or inaccurate, most of us believe the journalism we read and watch.)

Step 7   *Judging:* The consumer uses the product and judges whether it was all the stories said it was. If it's not, then the process shifts into reverse. The customer returns the product, tells friends and colleagues that it was a failure, feels that he's been duped, and might take action against the company by writing letters to the media or giving an interview to a reporter that is highly critical of the product.

At any step along the way, an unflattering media story can derail the process of building consumers' interest. A consumer might be ready to buy your product or an investor might be willing to devote some capital to your company, but until he completes that transaction, he is likely to change his mind if he reads some bad press.

These seven steps show how overlapping public relations initiatives can encourage consumers to test new products. However, the steps also demonstrate how public relations can work against a product or company that fails to live up to its stories. When reality doesn't match a company's public relations, the company develops a reputation for hype that will hurt its future publicity efforts. Reporters who believe that a company misled them into writing a *puff piece* won't cover your next development or, even worse, they will punish the company by writing a negative story. By following the Foundational Rules for Public Relations Success that I outline in this book, you will understand how to present the facts about your company to the media with confidence and accuracy.

Know What Reporters Really Want

Rick Orlov, the highly regarded political reporter for the Los Angeles *Daily News*, tells a story about a disgruntled reader who called one day to complain about one of his stories. The reader accused Rick of intentional bias. The conversation went as follows:

> "I know just what you were thinking when you wrote that story," the reader said.
>
> "I bet you don't," Rick said.
>
> "You were thinking, 'I'm going to get those guys,'" the reader said.
>
> "Actually," said Rick, "I was thinking, 'As soon as I finish this story, I can go home.'"

This says it all. What reporters really want is usually pretty simple: They want their calls returned, they want a quote for their story, and they want to do their job and go home. Don't make your relationship with reporters complicated.

Reporters' motives are simple: They want to produce a good story and then they want to go home.

Not All Stories Are Created Equal

When you begin seeking press coverage, don't leap at every chance to be included in a story. In many cases, if a reporter's proposed story angle doesn't fit in with your company's strategic public relations plan, it's better to pass on the opportunity.

If a potential client came to you and wanted to buy your company's services, and if you found out that that client had a poor credit history, along with a reputation for suing its vendors, you probably wouldn't be interested in signing them up. Use the same discretion with your PR.

When it comes to press opportunities, executives often forget that quality *is more important than* quantity.

When I was vice president of public relations for an Internet company, the NASDAQ began falling and, as with many public high-tech companies, the value of stock options began taking a nose-dive. A reporter called me because she was doing a story about low employee morale related to the sinking worth of stock options.

A public relations professional who operated under the assumption that she should grab any press opportunity would have granted the interview. However, my company was not yet publicly held and, according to the valuations assigned by top-tier investment banks, our stock option price was still stable. At that moment, it would have been misguided to give investors the sense that our morale was declining when, in fact, we were still doing well. I told the reporter we didn't fit the story angle and, as a result, we missed out on a chance to have our company's name in the paper, but we also avoided being lumped in with less fortunate companies.

Measure Your Pain Threshold

Any credible story is sure to include something you would have left out if you were writing the story. If, for example, your stock was at an all-time low six months ago, but today it's at an all-time high, it is a pretty sure bet that the story will mention that and speculate as to whether the high can hold. If the company's past CEO resigned after a sexual harassment scandal, then it's a given that the negative history is going to be retold in the story, even if today's CEO has presided over a positive change in the company's culture.

Before you move forward, take an accurate, no-holds-barred measurement of your company's pain threshold. If the company would consider it a failure if the story were to mention any glitch from the past, then don't try to get a story published because you will only end up failing.

> *Media stories are not company brochures. If you only want a puff piece, then write it yourself and give it to your customers. If you want your story to appear in the mass media, then you need to be prepared to do an interview where you might have to answer some challenging questions.*

No publication or broadcast program wants to be known for doing puff pieces and any story must have the essential element of drama. Therefore, a story about a high-flying company will ask the question, "Can it last?" A story about a political candidate who is leading in the polls will pose the question, "But is there any momentum behind the candidate?"

It's a reporter's job to be skeptical, to ask the tough questions, and to set up the drama. Often, business people think that when a reporter is asking tough questions, he is, in effect, sticking a knife into the company. As a former reporter, I can tell you that it's fine for a journalist to take a few jabs at your company, but what you want to avoid is having that reporter stab you in the back. See Chapters 9 through 11 for more detailed advice on how to avoid being stabbed in the back by remaining calm, nondefensive, and sticking to the facts.

Comedy also can be an element of a story that some executives might find difficult to take. Recently, one of my clients was the focus of a story that started with a joke. My client didn't think the joke was funny and assumed that the reporter was intentionally making his company a laughingstock. On the contrary, every outsider who read the story chuckled at the joke and believed that the company was favorably covered in the story.

A story that is generally accurate but points out a wart or two will actually appear more credible than a story that's purely positive; furthermore, it may result in increased business for your company. This fact is even more apparent in business journalism because business reporters are, on the whole, tougher, smarter, and more sophisticated than their general assignment counterparts. Their stories will turn over all the rocks and expose past history, but ultimately, most U.S. business publications and programs like to celebrate capitalism and corporate successes.

The Alpha Dog Story Leads the Pack

When an editor assigns a story about a company to a reporter, the first move the reporter makes is to seek out everything that has ever been written about that company. The Internet has made that process very easy. At some of the larger newspapers, magazines, and TV news shows, the reporter calls the in-house librarian and orders a Lexis-Nexis search. If the resulting research turns up unflattering facts, such as a pattern of unscrupulous business practices and faulty merchandise, it's a given that the reporter will mention those old accusations in her new story.

Moreover, it doesn't matter if the company has changed or if new management is in charge.

The first story written about the company is the Alpha Dog Story, and the Alpha Dog leads the pack. Therefore, it is absolutely essential to any company that you take your time securing that all-important Alpha Dog Story, as it will determine your company's coverage for years to come.

Often, when an executive decides that he wants to inaugurate a public relations program, he thinks that he should see results—in the form of a flattering front-page story in *The New York Times* or *The Wall Street Journal*. However, it takes systematic strategy to define your story and find the right reporter to tell it.

One of my clients, an entrepreneur who made a fortune in the early days of the Internet boom, came to me for help soon after he was severely bitten by an Alpha Dog Story. He had sold most of his Internet businesses at the height of the market, making him one of the lucky few who profited by the high-tech bubble of the late-1990s. By the time he had formed his new company, the Internet boom had gone bust, investors had lost their money, and employees had gotten pink slips. Even worse, the very reporters who had written reams of enthusiastic stories about even the flimsiest Internet plays, were trying to explain what happened to all that money. Many of those reporters were angry at having been misled by companies and now they were out to set the record straight by being tougher on their story subjects.

Unfortunately, the entrepreneur was used to getting flattering coverage from his Internet ventures, and he figured that winning streak would continue and help to fuel his new company. When a reporter he didn't know called him, saying that he wanted to do a story on the entrepreneur's post-Internet life, the entrepreneur jumped at the chance. He gave the reporter an intimate level of access, inviting the journalist to shadow him as he met with potential investors and supervised the construction of his new house in the most expensive zip code in Los Angeles.

The resulting story was a disaster. The entrepreneur was quoted saying all kinds of things that he wished he hadn't said about how much money he made, his liquidity, and his rich and famous neighbors. The story ended up being a psychological autopsy of the go-go Internet Age, with the entrepreneur starring as the poster child of greed. Worse, it became the Alpha Dog Story about his new company. From that point forward, reporters who contemplated writing about the entrepreneur would uncover that story in their first five minutes of research.

Overcoming a Bad Alpha Dog Story

There are ways to overcome a bad Alpha Dog Story. But first, recognize that stories have a long life. Expect reporters to ask about the earlier reports and be prepared to answer their questions nondefensively, while emphasizing the positive aspects of the new company.

Beggars Are Never Happy

The next lesson is that pitching a story doesn't mean pushing it. If you call up a journalist, pitch your story to the best of your ability, and get turned down, you must then let it go.

Remember that you are not looking for just any story; you are looking for the right story. If you push and prod and persuade until the reporter gives in, chances are that you won't be happy with the published result.

One CEO of a public company decided that a story in a major financial newspaper could help him mount a secondary stock offering. He ordered his director of public relations to get a reporter interested and made it clear that the director's job depended on it.

The public relations director called and pitched the story. The reporter wasn't interested. But the director of public relations didn't relent because his job depended on it. Finally, after weeks of phone calls, the reporter agreed. When the story was published, it centered on the company's short-term debt and featured the comments of one analyst who had recently downgraded the company's stock, ignoring six other analysts' favorable reports. The CEO got his story, and the public relations director got to keep his job, but the secondary offering was a bust.

The moral of this story is a bit like the refrain in the Garth Brooks song that sometimes, it's best to be thankful for unanswered prayers.

Reporters Are Not Your Friends

Nor are reporters your enemies, but you must bear in mind that they tell stories for a living—they don't write corporate brochures.

For a story to get into print or on the air, it must raise nearly as many questions as it answers. Just because the reporter meets you for lunch and laughs at your jokes doesn't mean that she is going to ignore the basic laws of journalism.

For example, if your earnings exceeded expectations, a journalist might wonder in print whether you can sustain that track record. If the board is so happy with your performance that it approves a record bonus, then a journalist could target you as an example of corporate greed. If your employees hunker down whenever you walk through the office, the journalist might focus on morale issues.

None of these potential landmines mean that you should abandon your plans to get into the public eye. After all, if a reporter scrutinizes your company, poses the tough questions, and writes a fair and balanced account, the result, most likely, will be a story that brings you and your company the kind of credibility you cannot buy.

The New York Times Equals *The Santa Monica Daily Press*

This is a basic mistake that is easily avoidable if you understand how many journalists start their careers: *The New York Times* is seldom the first stop on a reporter's resume. Most reporters start by working somewhere else that's much smaller. For example, before I covered national news for *USA Today*, I worked at the *Fairfax Journal*, where I wrote about local news such as hospital funding and animal control.

Many people make the mistake of treating reporters from small outlets as though they are less important than reporters from more prestigious outlets. However, that beginning reporter from The Santa Monica Daily Press *is probably going to move up in the world. And when he gets to* The New York Times, *do you want him to remember you as the person who treated him poorly?*

Furthermore, trade magazines, small town papers, and local broadcasts are all fodder for national news. Therefore, while reporters for *The New York Times* get exclusives and break the big stories of the day, they also frequently pick up story ideas from reading other reporters' work. In addition, when national news reporters decide to do a story, they first research the topic. Their research often turns up the stories that have appeared in smaller outlets and markets. Those stories can set the tone for coverage in the national media.

Phony Is Baloney

Speaking of credibility, don't go out of your way to show off just because a reporter comes to call. Hyperbole is fine—in a piece of art. But in the realm of journalism, the only thing hyperbole accomplishes is to make you look bad.

For example, dot-coms lost a lot of credibility because their executives kept making grandiose pronouncements to the press, such as, "We have no competition because we're the only company doing X, Y, and Z in precisely that order" and "We're next-generation." These proclamations intrigued reporters the first few dozen times they heard them, but after that reporters just made fun of such statements.

Reporters have an innate sense that I call the *Bull Detector*. Alarms go off in their heads when a source says something that just doesn't add up. The Bull Detector also registers when an executive acts like a presiding monarch instead of a regular guy. For this reason, I advise all my clients to place the call themselves when they phone a reporter. Unless you are Jack Welch, reporters think it's pompous when a secretary calls them and says, "Please hold for Ms. So-and-So returning your call." They make fun of you with their colleagues and some of that contempt is bound to seep into the next story they write about your company.

The Bull Detector does its most serious work when an executive fudges the facts.

If you lie to a reporter, then you deserve the crummy coverage that is sure to follow.

You Can't Pitch What You Don't Know

One of the things that irritates reporters more than anything is to get a pitch call from someone who doesn't know their publication and doesn't know what the reporter covers. There is simply no point in calling a reporter who covers legal affairs and asking them to cover a movie premiere. Before you pick up the phone, do a little research.

There are plenty of databases you can subscribe to that give listings of publications and broadcast outlets, the reporters who work there and what they cover. That is a good way to start, but you can't rely solely on those databases. Do your homework: Check out the media outlet's web site, buy a copy or two of the publication, and read the reporter's past stories and get a feel for what a particular reporter is interested in covering.

You don't have to be a know-it-all about the story you are pitching. Know the basic facts and be able to answer the questions you can expect. However, if a reporter asks something you don't know the answer to, then use it as an opening to say something like, "That's something I am sure our CEO, Mr. So-and-So, would love to talk with you about. Do you want me to see if he can give you a call this afternoon so you can get a better feel for the story before you pitch it to your editor?"

The ground rules I have discussed in this chapter all serve as a starting point for the media training lessons that follow in the chapters ahead. These basic tenets also outline how journalism and public relations complement and conflict with each other. Knowing how you can avoid conflict and focus your attention on helping a reporter get his story will, in the long run, help your company achieve public relations success.

Key Points

➤ Understanding how public relations and the media work empowers you to define your company's story and shape your public image.

➤ The first story about your company sets the tone for coverage for years to come.

➤ Reporters' wants are generally simple: They want to produce an interesting story, meet their deadline, and go home.

➤ Reporters from local outlets are just as important to your media success as national correspondents.

➤ Don't leap at every story opportunity. Quality journalism will benefit your company more than quantity. Don't push a journalist to do a piece on your company.

➤ Accurate stories benefit companies much more than puff pieces.

➤ Stories must have drama for readers to read them, and drama often means tension.

➤ Beware of reporters' built-in Bull Detector.

HOMEWORK

➤ Write a 100-word description of the Alpha Dog Story about your company that you would like to read in print.

➤ Measure your pain threshold by compiling a list of the negatives about your company. Is there much competition in your product sector? Does your company have high debt? Has the company filed for or emerged from bankruptcy? Have sales declined?

CHAPTER

2

How Journalists
Think and Behave

Lesson Plan

*In this chapter, we look at a reporter's workload and discuss
how a reporter's day-to-day life affects the stories he or she
generates. Understanding the deadline pressures journalists
routinely work under can help you work with them more effectively. Journalists often employ a sense of fair play that I call
Kindergarten Justice. I'll show you how to make it work to
your advantage. Finally, I'll cover the importance of avoiding
the words "no comment."*

They come into your office, asking question after question. No
subject is too personal for them to stick their noses—and
their notebooks—into. They act like they have all the power
in your relationship with them. To your face, they'll act like your
friend. But they can turn on a dime. If you say you can't talk about

27

a particular deal, they'll darkly hint that they'll have to point out in their story that you are evasive. If you ask them to turn off the camera, they nod their heads and keep on shooting. Should you ask them a question about their life or career, their answer would not reveal much of anything. And when your interview is over, they will call your worst enemies, interview them, and put their quotes alongside yours in the story.

It is easy to dislike journalists. That is, if you don't understand them.

Beginning with the next chapter, you will learn how to apply what you learn here about a reporter's job pressures. You will see how understanding what motivates reporters and editors will aid you in pitching your company's story. First, you need to understand that, while journalism can be fun and glamorous, there is much stress that goes with the job.

> *The truth is, reporters and producers do not have an easy life. Once you understand this, it will be easier for you to work with them, enjoy them, and benefit from your relationship with them.*

Generally, news professionals are the kind of people that many people want to befriend. Journalists are interesting because they know a little bit about a lot of subjects. After all, the day before they came to interview you, they might have been reporting on the latest trial of the century or test-driving the latest hot car or covering a union lock-down.

Journalists have an inside story on whatever everybody is talking about. They are smart and hardworking, and they are not motivated by money. The Peter Jennings of the journalism world rake in millions, but there aren't many people in that income category out there. Print reporters fresh out of school probably earn less than $30,000 a year. After years of work, few will make it into the major leagues and those who do probably won't earn too far into the six figures. TV journalists used to be the financial envy of print reporters, but that was before the rise of cable and Internet news created many more lower paying jobs. Now, local TV reporters aren't compensated much more than their print counterparts. Indeed, journalism is becoming a pink-collar ghetto—and when women begin to dominate a profession, salaries deflate.

There is little hope that the future is going to put much more in their pocketbooks. When an economic downturn affects advertising, you can bet that reporters will feel it as well. Since the dot-com crash, major magazine editors have seen their compensation reduced by as much as 25 percent. In a good year, 4 percent raises are the norm and, in journalism, there is rarely such a thing as an annual bonus. Even at newspapers that are protected by union wage-and-hour guidelines, there is little respect for those who work a mere eight hours a day. A reporter who is gung-ho about assuming more work is rewarded with plenty more of it. Overtime pay? Nice idea, but not a widespread reality.

Why Journalists Choose This Career

If it is not for the money, then why do journalists choose their profession? For one, on most days, it is fun. You aren't stuck in an office all day because you are out conducting interviews and photo shoots. You get to pick up the phone and talk to pretty much whomever you want. When big stories break, you get to be in the middle of the action, which makes for a great adrenaline rush.

Journalists are important because they inform the public and don't have to answer to anyone except their editor. People mostly enter journalism because they like to write or they enjoy the creative process of putting words and video together to tell a story.

Many reporters and producers want to be a watchdog on our government and those in power. They want to help protect the little guy. They want to tell a good story and they don't want to have to play games to get it. And yes, they want the truth.

However, sometimes, journalists have to settle on just reporting the facts, and there are times when the facts and the truth are two very different things. Take the example of one of my clients, an attorney who specializes in white-collar criminal defense, particularly in technology industries. He once represented a company that manufactured hammers for the military. When the manufacturer sent the bill for the hammers to the Department of Defense, the government filed criminal and civil charges against the company. The crime was the fact that the hammers cost $1,500 each.

Because of the outrageous price, one could easily jump to the conclusion that the company was cheating the government. However, this one fact doesn't tell the full story. The truth was that the government's own requirements and specifications, including the costly and impractical tests that the government contractually obligated the manufacturer to perform, were the major reasons underlying the price. As I'll explain later in this chapter, because reporters are frequently pressed for time in producing their stories, a situation such as this, in which the appearance and the facts are vastly mismatched, could potentially be dangerous.

Reporters Look for Drama

In addition to the fact that the facts can be misleading, there are also biases that can affect journalists' work. *Bias*, a book by former CBS news veteran Bernard Goldberg, makes a strong case that the people who make up the U.S. news media are predominately liberal and, therefore, the media's news coverage leans toward the liberal end of the political spectrum. It's not that the media intends to be derogatory or dismissive of conservatives; it's just that media people think their way of looking at issues is reasonable. Moreover, in every aspect of their lives, they are surrounded by other media people, who they also think are reasonable and who hold similar opinions.

In addition to working together, many reporters tend to live in the same neighborhoods and therefore socialize with other editors, producers, and reporters. Their ideas of what is reasonable are therefore reinforced by their neighbors and colleagues.

There's a lot to what Mr. Goldberg says, but the people who report the news don't think so much in terms of liberal and conservative. Instead, reporters are always looking for the drama, the excitement, the *news* of a situation. For example, any reporter assigned to do a story on the beautiful new concert hall in town is also going to include interviews with the antidevelopment group that tried to halt the project. If a reporter is going to do a story on the fastest business expansion in history, he is going to include quotes from experts who warn that it can't last. If a reporter is doing a story on $1,500 hammers, he might find out how many hammers you could buy with $1,500 at the local Home Depot.

In the case of the hammers, the manufacturer didn't help the situation because instead of explaining why the same hammer might cost $20 at Home Depot, the company spokesperson simply said "no comment" (more about that later). He didn't let the reporter know the rest of the facts: That the government's hammer required the manufacturer to perform hundreds of separate and distinct tests and hire a panel of Ph.D.s, greatly inflating the cost of the hammer. Without knowing these important facts, a journalist covering the story might resort to *Kindergarten Justice*—part of journalists' watchdog mission to expose wrongdoing and unfairness.

Journalists believe that the world should play fair,
good guys should win, and bad guys should go to jail. They
see it as their duty to ensure that rich and powerful people
are held accountable for their actions and reprimanded
should they become arrogant. This is Kindergarten Justice.

Remember, journalism is called *The Fourth Estate* for a reason—reporters truly perceive themselves as the watchdogs in the corridors of power; guarding truth, justice, and the American way; and they have, indeed, exposed corruption and wrongdoing throughout history. Upton Sinclair uncovered the disgusting conditions in the meat-packing industry; Bob Woodward and Carl Bernstein bared the lies that infected a presidency; and, within the past two years, dozens of reporters uncovered the deceptive accounting practices employed by companies like Enron and Tyco that cost thousands of investors their life savings.

However, sometimes, a reporter states that someone is doing something out of the norm and that a reasonable person in the same situation would do things differently. As a result, the person at the center of a controversial story is seen and portrayed as suspicious. For example, let's consider JonBenet Ramsey and the ensuing scandal surrounding the mystery of her death. Ramsey's parents hired a lawyer who limited investigators' access to the family. The press widely interpreted this as an action akin to pleading guilty. The reporters and experts on TV shows like *Larry King Live* and *On the Record with Greta Van Susteren* kept saying things like, "Well, if it were my daughter who was murdered, I would have camped out at the Police Department and demanded that they give me a polygraph test. I wouldn't have done what the Ramseys did."

Keep in mind that many of the reporters making these pronouncements had no experience with losing a child. Moreover, besides attending to their own grief, the Ramseys had other children to protect and a company full of employees who were dependent on John Ramsey for their paychecks. Many other business owners would have handled the situation the same way the Ramseys did to protect their children and employees, but it was much easier for the press to rely on pure Kindergarten Justice to heighten the drama in the story.

The Ramseys' decision not to offer explanation for their behavior opened the door for commentators and reporters to draw conclusions and that cemented the public's perceptions. Their reputation never recovered.

Kindergarten Justice can work in your favor, also. For example, you might have a story if the Department of Transportation in your city is constantly closing down access to parking meters in front of your store—but the store down the street has never been inconvenienced in the same way, and it happens to be owned by the mayor's daughter.

Kindergarten Justice is the reason reporters and editors love stories about shoplifting actresses, as I will discuss in the next chapter. In Kindergarten Justice logic, millionaires who shoplift deserve to be exposed, as do senators who constantly espouse "family values" but who are subsequently discovered to be carrying on an affair.

The Downside of Reporting and How It Affects Businesspeople

Understanding how reporters live at the mercy of the news will help you to communicate with them effectively. When big stories break, reporters have to drop their lives. It doesn't matter if it is their child's first birthday party or their parents' golden anniversary. Nothing matters except getting the story—especially to an assignment editor.

Once, when I was a reporter, covering the west for *USA Today*, there was an explosion in Nevada. My editor called to tell me to rush to the airport. So I did. But at certain times of the year, Los Angeles is subject to heavy fog—the kind that grounds airplanes. I called my editor:

"Are you there yet?" he asked.

"No. The airport is fogged in," I said.

"But we have a deadline in an hour," he said.

"If I drive, it will take seven or eight hours," I said.

"But it's just an inch or two away on the map," he said.

"I can't help it—they've closed the airport," I said.

"Well, just get there," he said.

In that editor's mind, it didn't matter that the FAA or the weather was to blame for me not getting to the story in time for the deadline. *I* wasn't going to get there; *I* was going to miss the story.

*Ultimately, reporters are always at the mercy
of someone else. Their own needs, their own family
responsibilities, and their own schedules don't matter
in the pursuit of a story. This kind of illogical demand
creates a great deal of anxiety—and this anxiety manifests
itself in all kinds of ways, with potentially negative
ramifications for businesspeople.*

First, if you call reporters to pitch a story, they have so much work to do that it's always easier for them to say no. In addition, if they call you to get your cooperation on a story, it means they are already planning to write about your company or your industry and they have to get the interview immediately because their editor is breathing down their neck.

In addition to reporters' anxiety, during the past decade, their workload has increased exponentially. In the old days, a reporter assigned to cover a major story for a national newspaper would be expected to file a story every day. These expectations changed when the news cycle expanded. During the O. J. Simpson criminal trial, when I was reporting for *USA Today*, I was responsible for turning in a story by noon every day for the newspaper's international edition. By 5 P.M. I had to turn in a story detailing the day's court action—even if the court session hadn't concluded. Often, I would be expected to complement that story with a short companion piece, called a "sidebar," that spotlighted a side issue. Back then, that workload was considerable. Today, it would be just the beginning.

Nowadays, in addition to writing or producing pieces for their papers or broadcasts, reporters also have to come up with contributions for their organizations' web sites. A reporter for *NBC Nightly News*, for example, might be required to develop a story for the traditional broadcast, another for the web site, another for CNBC or MSNBC and might even be required to appear the next morning on *The Today Show*, usually without any extra compensation.

Pay is just one part of the problem. When journalists talk to other journalists, they admit that they are not well prepared to cover the most significant issues facing the country.

In 2002, the Foundation for American Communications (FACS), a nonprofit journalism education organization, polled 401 randomly selected broadcast journalists, newspaper journalists, and publishers from a national cross section of media outlets. The poll showed the following:

- The overall quality of reporting is rated by 56 percent as a three on a scale of one to five, where five means excellent and one means poor.

- Journalists' preparation for covering the most important national issues is rated by 75 percent as a three on a scale of one to five, where five means excellent and one means poor.

These statistics didn't surprise me. I think that after a few years, journalists feel frustrated at the constantly growing workload and the constantly shrinking time allowed to understand, research, and sink their teeth into a story.

Considering the lifestyle, it's no surprise that after a few years, your everyday, working journalist can begin to feel victimized and just plain tired. After years of reporting "breakthrough," "first," "last," and "unprecedented" events, they start to become cynical.

In summary, understanding the pressures reporters face and their ways of looking at the world will help you to communicate with them effectively.

KEY POINTS

➤ Reporters choose this profession because they see themselves as serving society and exposing wrongdoings.

➤ Reporters workloads and lifestyles often creeps into their coverage; knowing how they work helps you respond effectively.

(continued)

KEY POINTS *(Continued)*

➤ Reporters are not motivated by money.

➤ Kindergarten Justice is shorthand for the way a reporter often looks at the world to determine what is fair and what is not.

➤ Reporters look for the drama within every story.

➤ As the Internet and 24-hour cable news channels have turned news into a 24-hour business, reporters have seen their workload increase exponentially and without additional compensation. The increased stress that results can affect the way your company is covered.

HOMEWORK

➤ Pick out a local business reporter and track the stories that he or she does for one month. How many stories are there? How many people are quoted in each story? This will give you an idea of how much work the reporter has done in a relatively short time frame.

Responding to Journalists

Lesson Plan

Reporters do not have an easy lifestyle, as I explained in the previous chapter. You can take a number of proactive steps for making journalists' jobs easier, as I'll discuss in this chapter.

The first thing reporters do when they get an assignment is a quick round of research. Simultaneously, they scroll through their list of contacts and make phone calls to anyone anywhere who might have any scrap of information that can help them get the story.

Every second, their deadline is getting closer and reporters who miss deadlines are committing the number-one sin of journalism. You can ease a reporter's anxiety just by returning his phone calls. You don't even have to give a reporter the interview right away. Tell him that you are tied up with something, but you can call him back in a few minutes. This will buy you a few minutes to gather your thoughts and to ensure that your interview is optimal.

Even if you're not the best source on the story, call back anyway. At worst, you'll have nothing to contribute to the story, but at least you will be responsive to the reporter's need to meet his deadline. At best, you might be able to refer the reporter to a better-placed source thereby building a future ally.

It's not that complicated when it comes to understanding what reporters need and want from you. They want the story, they want it in time to make their deadline, and they don't want you to lie, but if you do, they want to catch you in a whopper.

Back in the 1980s, some reporters asked then-Colorado Senator Gary Hart if he was unfaithful to his wife. Hart, who, at that point, was a frontrunner among the candidates vying to be the next Democratic party presidential nominee, told the press that he wasn't. Then he said that if the reporters didn't believe him, they could follow him. Within a few weeks, there were front-page photos of Senator Hart canoodling with a pretty young woman who was not his wife.

This story reminds me of the fable about the frog and the scorpion. The scorpion convinces the frog to carry him across the stream. The frog is skeptical because the scorpion is known to be a not-very-nice guy and his sting is deadly, but the scorpion promises not to sting and the frog is kindly, so off they sail. The moment they reach the other side, the scorpion stings his benefactor: As the frog dies, he asks why the scorpion would do this after all his promises. The scorpion replies, "Because I'm a scorpion."

Reporters are reporters. Don't dare them to turn your life upside down and investigate you and your family from every angle. Most likely, they'll find something they can speculate on and analyze.

For instance, how many of us have a relative who has done something embarrassing? How many of us have acted inappropriately in public and made a spectacle of ourselves, or got arrested for our part in a college prank? Don't issue a dare to a reporter; he'll take it as a challenge.

Treat Reporters Like Human Beings

Another thing you can do to make a reporter's life easier is to be polite. Offer her a glass of water or a cup of coffee when she arrives at your office. If you validate parking for clients, offer to validate hers. (Some reporters might insist on paying for their parking, but offer anyway.) In other words, treat every reporter with respect.

Here's an example of what not to do. In the very beginning of the O. J. Simpson murder saga, his attorney, Robert Shapiro, called a press conference at his office. Dozens of reporters arrived at his building—a fancy glass skyscraper in Century City, where the parking fee maxed out at $20. We were directed into a ground-floor conference room that was empty except for a podium. There were only six chairs so most of us sat on the floor. Shapiro was then 40 minutes late. Finally, at the end of the press conference, we headed for the door but we were told we couldn't go out the front door; we were directed to a back exit. On the way back to the parking lot, there was much grumbling about being treated like animals.

Shapiro's relationship with the press never recovered. I'm sure he felt the snubbing and that might have played a part in his decision to send about a dozen reporters a Christmas present of a bottle of a new perfume by Bijan called, appropriately, DNA. Most recipients sent it back without even so much as a note. Many reporters then published stories about how Shapiro had insulted the press by ignoring the fact that reporters aren't allowed to accept gifts from players in their stories.

Shapiro was treated as more and more irrelevant. Most reporters ignored him and went straight to Johnnie Cochran whenever they needed a defense team quote. In contrast to Shapiro,

Cochran always had a smile, and he always remembered your name. When a reporter went to his office, he didn't have to use the back door. Cochran was always late for interviews, but once he entered the room, he was so charming that reporters didn't mind the wait. He returned phone calls and would answer questions. He never told reporters anything spontaneously, but he always made them look good to their editors because he would always call them back.

Treating a reporter like a human being doesn't mean that you are going to receive preferential treatment. It doesn't mean that a reporter is going to put your interests above his ethical interpretations of how he needs to cover the story. It does mean that a little bit of good will can go a long way, and if you treat a reporter fairly, he is more likely to listen to your side of the story and to present it fairly.

From time to time, a new client comes to me after receiving particularly harsh treatment in print or on air. Invariably, the client will tell me, "but during the interview, the reporter was so nice. I really thought he liked me."

I always say the same thing: "The reporter probably did like you. I am sure he meant all the nice things he said. But when the interview is over, friendship takes a back seat. The only loyalty a true journalist feels is to the story."

In other words, don't get caught up in the fantasy of having a deep friendship with a reporter you have known for an hour. You are not there to make a friend. You want to get your story out to the journalist's audience.

Remember that a journalist is trying to tell a fair story, not promote your agenda. Therefore, your goal should never be to have the reporter generate a puff piece about you and your company; it wouldn't appear credible.

Finally, being pleasant to a reporter will not make him less likely to call attention to a lie. When something you say just doesn't sound quite believable, any reporter is likely to double-check that fact. This is often the difference between a story that helps you achieve your strategic goals and a story that hurts.

Don't Accept a Reporter's Bad Behavior

Being respectful toward reporters doesn't mean that you should accept unprofessional behavior. This is where I draw a hard line. Many public relations (PR) professionals are so afraid of incurring a reporter's wrath that they will accept any kind of behavior from a reporter; I don't.

I expect reporters to do fair and accurate reporting. They don't have to interpret the facts and reach the same conclusions as I and my clients do, but they have an obligation to report the facts fully and fairly, which includes giving us our say. They also have an obligation to act professionally and if not to be kind, then at least to be nonthreatening.

I expect journalists to adhere to their professional code of ethics, meaning reporters can't report innuendo unless it is clearly stated as their perception, not fact, and as long as the subject of the innuendo is allowed an opportunity to respond.

Facts aren't what they used to be in journalism. When I was studying journalism at the University of Florida, a fact error in a story meant failing the assignment. My professors weren't interested in hearing explanations, and they showed no mercy. When I was reporting for *USA Today*, a fact error in a story caused the toughest reporters to cry and managing editors to write front-page apologies to our readers.

However, today, in the instant-news-instant-analysis era of 24-hour news cycles, the stigma of reporting a fact error has all but disappeared. Remember the Sniper case of 2002? Throughout the three-week siege, when the sniper was randomly gunning down innocent people, reporters repeated a myriad of factual errors, including that the sniper was in a white van, that the sniper stole a credit card from a victim at a liquor store heist in Alabama, and that there was no tie to terrorism.

As we all know now, there was no white van, there was no credit card stolen from a victim in Alabama, but there was a tenuous tie to terrorism because the sniper had told acquaintances that he was sympathetic to the 9/11 terrorists. Regardless, there was no mea culpa from the media. Instead, TV anchors told their audiences that when you report the news so fast, there are bound to be mistakes. While the media is more tolerant of their own mistakes, they are less tolerant of anyone else's, simply because they have 24-hour news cycles to fill and they need the stories.

In mid-2003, when *New York Times* reporter Jayson Blair resigned after being found to have plagiarized or made up dozens of stories, including his sniper coverage, journalists became a bit more open to admitting that they are not perfect. But prior to that story breaking, sources who complained that Blair's stories were inaccurate had been disbelieved by the newsroom leaders. It took a scandal that threatened the trust on which the *Times'* brand is based to convince the newsroom managers to be a little less arrogant and defensive when a source complained.

When I was starting out in journalism, the adage, "Get it first, but first, get it right" was drilled into each fledgling reporter. Today, sometimes it seems that getting it first matters, but getting it wrong is no big deal—there is always another show to correct your misreporting in the form of an update.

Use Facts to Grab a Reporter's Attention

The best way to deal with journalists in almost any situation is to stick with the facts.

For example, a fact-checker for a major business magazine called me at 3 P.M. to enlist my help in getting one of my clients to verify facts in a story about his company. She needed to speak with him by noon the next day and the clock was ticking. Normally, this request would be a piece of cake. But there was one hurdle: My client was on a safari deep in Africa and without a cell phone.

My client's assistant and I went to work to get the fact-checker what she needed. We answered every question except for one. The only person who had the information the fact-checker needed was the executive on safari. We knew that in a few hours, the executive was to travel by horseback to a village, where he would board a chartered helicopter that would take him to an airport, the first leg of his long journey home. We arranged for a messenger to be at the helicopter with a telegram from me in hand, asking the CEO to call me immediately. If all went according to plan, the executive would be on the phone, verifying the story's facts at noon the next day and meeting the fact-checker's deadline.

Feeling victorious, I called the fact-checker to tell her the arrangements. To my surprise, she was not pleased. "I have a lunch scheduled," she said. "I don't see why he can't call me right now."

I took a deep breath. "There is no phone where he is," I told her. "I can't get a message to him any faster than this."

"Well, what about a satellite phone?"

I took another deep breath. "Even if he had a satellite phone, where he is there are no satellite receivers, so it wouldn't work," I said. "The fact is that we are meeting the deadline you gave me and he will be calling you. I don't know what to tell you about your lunch schedule, unless you want me to tell him to call you a few hours later, when he's changing planes."

"Do you want me to write in the story that the CEO was unavailable?" she threatened.

Saying the CEO was unavailable would have been the sort of innuendo that is usually not helpful to any company's public image when it appears in a story. Too, it was not compatible with the facts. I was not going to let her get away with it.

"That would be a fact error," I said calmly. "The facts are, you gave me a deadline for him to call you and we will meet that deadline.

We have demonstrated that we will go to great lengths to work with you. Those are the facts and if you state it as otherwise, that is unprofessional and unethical journalism."

She chose to reschedule her lunch, and I reinforced my belief that stating the facts really works with reporters. This lesson comes to mind frequently.

Respond to Journalists in a Fact-Based Way

Journalists respond to the facts; therefore, beat them to the punch by being prepared. When I represented a company whose goods were manufactured in Asia, stories about substandard working conditions in developing countries were in the news every day. As much as the CEO wanted positive recognition for his company's record earnings, it was a given that he would face questions about manufacturing practices and whether his company was guilty of abuses. Reporters would ask simply because it was a hot topic and because it was public information that my client manufactured goods overseas.

Knowing that we would face detailed questions about the company's treatment of its employees overseas, the first thing we did was make a list of the facts. They were as follows:

- The company was a founding member of an industry watchdog group and adhered to the group's standards.
- The company worked only with factories that allowed independent inspections and verifications of working conditions.
- The company had never been cited by any group for violating working conditions.
- The CEO and each member of his senior team—individually and without warning—visited and inspected their subcontracting factories twice a year.

Armed with these facts, the CEO could answer any question that any journalist posed about working conditions in overseas factories.

Never Say "No Comment"

Here's another reason why this fact-based approach works with the press: Journalists have to ask tough questions—that is their job. Generally, their questions don't make it into their stories but your answers do. This is one reason why you should never say "no comment" to a reporter.

When you say "no comment" to a journalist,
you are drawing a line in the sand. You are letting
the journalist speak for your company instead of
capitalizing on an opportunity to share your
message directly with the audience.

For example, let's say that CEO Jones is in an interview that goes like this:

Reporter: "There have been a lot of reports lately about factories in Asia where the workers are abused and paid less than a dollar a day for making your products, which retail here in the United States for $60. What do you have to say about that?"

CEO: "No comment."

Reporter: "Isn't your company named in a lawsuit about the substandard working conditions?"

CEO: "No comment."

The average person would look at this exchange and deduce that the company is guilty. It is true that appearance and reality aren't always the same, but in the media, appearance readily masquerades as fact. The reporter, when writing the story, is going to say something like, "CEO Jones refused to comment on allegations of abuse at his company's Asian factory. He also said, 'No comment' when asked about the lawsuit against his company by Nonprofit Public Interest Group X. But So-and-So from Public Interest Group X says that is because CEO Jones has a lot to hide." If the story is on TV, you can bet that piece of reporting will be followed with video of heinous working conditions in some foreign factory that might not even be one making CEO Jones's products.

Now let's look at a better approach:

Reporter: "There have been a lot of reports lately about factories in Asia where the workers are abused and paid less than a dollar a day for making your products, which retail here in the United States for $60. What do you have to say about that?"

CEO: "You know, these reports concern me because the people that put their faith in our products deserve to know that our products are made with the highest standards, both in the quality of the product and the quality of the way we treat the people who make our products. And that is why it is so important for you to know that we helped to found the industry watchdog group and we adhere to all of their standards. As a matter of fact, those standards exceed the standards outlined not only in international law but in the law of the countries in which we operate."

Reporter: "But isn't your company named in a lawsuit about the substandard working conditions?"

CEO: "I'm not aware of any lawsuit but even if I were, you know that I couldn't comment on any specific pending legal matter. What I can tell you is that our customers need to know that we take this issue seriously, to the point that we work only with factories that allow independent inspections and verifications of working conditions. And, as a matter of fact, I go there twice every year, unannounced, to see for myself that our factories are good, safe places to work. Because of the jobs we provide, we are helping the economy in that country and helping people to earn a better way of life for them and for their families."

As you can see from these examples, there is just no debate when it comes to "no comment." When journalists hear "no comment," they think that you're trying to hide something important, and that perception is sure to show up in the story.

The truth is that there is always *something* you can say to journalists. If you are asked about a legal case filed against your company, you could say, "It is company policy to not comment on pending legal matters, but what I can say is that when all the facts are in, our company is going to be shown as deserving of our leadership in the marketplace."

**Whenever you are tempted to say, "no comment,"
immediately try to think of what you CAN say.**

For example, let's look at the following scenario:

REPORTER: "What do you think about your CEO being led from the office in handcuffs today?"

SPOKESPERSON: "That was a really sad moment for all of us. But once all the facts are known, I am confident that our company will get back to doing what we do best: satisfying our customers and building the best widgets in the world."

The spokesperson could have said "no comment." Certainly, what he did say didn't shed any more light on any aspect of the case than if he had said those two forbidden words. Instead, he gave the reporter something to quote that didn't hurt his company and, in fact, might have made it look better.

Some lawyers insist on ordering spokespeople to say "no comment." (The lawyers are always in charge when a company is in a crisis.) Even if your lawyer is insisting that you respond "no comment," you can still find something more to say. For example, if your company has been wrongly accused of a crime, you might follow this response from a spokeswoman about a lawsuit against her company: She said, "It is our policy to say 'no comment' about any pending lawsuit, especially one as ludicrous as this one." She didn't say any-thing. But she said plenty.

Show Enthusiasm for Your Company and Your Product

It is easy to get along with reporters. All you have to do is to call them back, have the facts at hand, treat them like human beings, and never, ever lie. While you are doing all of that, remember to never mistake reporters for your friends. They have a job to do, and their job is not to make you look good. Their job is to tell a story. They aren't going to select the quote that makes your company look its best, unless it's also the quote that best illustrates their story.

Reporters are aware that when they write a story about your company, it could help your bottom line, but they don't want to feel like they are writing a free advertisement. Journalists want to believe that what they are doing is telling their audience something impor-tant. Therefore, an executive who presents himself as being confi-dent and sincere, but not arrogant, has a head start on dealing well with the media.

Reporters also want to know that the executive likes what he does for a living and is excited about it. Making buckets of money simply isn't enough to excite a reporter; remember, they are not mo-tivated by money.

An executive needs to present himself as a true believer in his product and is someone who is convinced that his company benefits society in a new and different way.

In the early days of the Internet boom, I represented a high-speed Internet access company. Our message to the media was that we were changing the business world, because our affordable suite of products enabled small businesses to have the same kind of high-speed data communications that big companies had been able to afford for years.

Finally, because of our company, Mom-and-Pop businesses could go head-to-head with the big guys and have a chance of winning. That message, delivered by a CEO who genuinely was excited about empowering small businesses, resounded positively with reporters and the ensuing stories reflected it.

Simply put, reporters have a tough job to do and you don't have a whole lot of control over them, unless you own their media outlet. Even then, if you squelch a story, expect another reporter at another outlet to get tipped off and then they will run a story about how you tried to prevent the truth from coming out.

Stop trying to control reporters. Put your energy into controlling yourself, which is the topic of our next chapter.

KEY POINTS

➤ Never say, "no comment."

➤ Just as you should treat reporters with respect, they should be fair in their dealings with you. If you feel they have overstepped the boundaries, don't be afraid to speak up.

➤ Reporters respond to facts.

➤ You can't control reporters, but you can control your own behavior.

➤ Show enthusiasm for your product.

HOMEWORK

➤ Comb through your personal contacts to find a friend or acquaintance who is a former news reporter. (There are a lot of us out there.) Chances are that if you make a few calls to trusted business associates, you will find a former reporter in your community who will go to lunch with you and talk with you about their reporting experiences, lifestyle, and pressures. These insights will allow you to understand how reporters approach the job and how you can best work with them.

What Is News?

Lesson Plan

Learning how to attract reporters to cover your company means learning what reporters think news is. In this chapter, we examine the news judgment skills that journalists begin developing from the moment they walk into their first newsroom. We work on developing your own sense of news judgment so your story pitches are compelling. Also, this chapter provides a list of topics that reporters often find newsworthy, as well as a list of topics that are a hard sell. Use the lists, along with what you learned in Chapter 2 about reporters' lifestyles and workloads, to turn your story pitches into coverage.

One of my clients has an emergency communications business. The company's software enables school principals to alert parents to school emergencies within moments. One phone call allows the principal to send a voice mail to thousands of parents simultaneously.

The company's launch was instant news to reporters because the product embodied a basic element that reporters are interested in: personal security.

Especially in post-9/11 America, journalists are attracted to stories they judge to contain elements that affect the personal safety of their readers. Within days of starting to work with this company, I was able to book them on a business talk show. It wasn't my story pitching ability that got my client this coverage. It was because the producer immediately responded to this topic.

Before you start working with the media, you first need to understand what the media deems newsworthy. You only get one chance to make a first impression, so when you call a reporter who you have never met and you want to pitch them a specific story, the reporter is first determining if you really understand what a story is. This can affect your relationship with that reporter for a long time to come.

The first thing any journalist learns is
news judgment. Whether you are in journalism school,
or working your way up from the copy desk, you learn
that when a dog bites a man, nobody cares. But
when a man bites a dog—now, that is news.

News judgment isn't static, though, and as our society changes, so does the notion of what is newsworthy. Reporters and editors constantly argue over whether a story belongs on page one. They argue the point before the paper comes out and they continue arguing it when they have the benefit of 20/20 hindsight. Media critics weigh in on those decisions, chastising TV network executives for focusing too much on unseemly celebrity behavior instead of reporting about famines or legal intricacies or whatever the critics deem to be "real news."

When reporters get together socially, they tell stories about their stories, pitch each other story ideas that their editors have already rejected and then argue over the news merit of those imagined stories. News judgment discussions are fun for reporters, especially because the merit of any story can change from day to day or even hour to hour. For example, the first high-flying IPO of a dot-com company was judged to be news. By the thousandth time, the collective news judgment had moved on and the thousandth CEO was left without a headline to call his own.

There is an old saying in journalism: "News is whatever is happening in your editor's life." There's a lot of truth in that. For example, if the city editor of your local newspaper has a teenager who is stressing out over upcoming SATs, that editor is probably going to be receptive to a story about a company that has developed a new method of prepping students to ace the tests.

The Stories That Naturally Make News

Here are some ways to help you determine the newsworthiness of the story you want to pitch. If your story fits into any of the categories that follow, your story has a better chance of making it into the news. Being included on the list doesn't guarantee positive, front-page coverage, but it does mean that you can most likely find a reporter somewhere who would be interested in doing the story:

- *Big money:* The bigger the pot of money on the table, the bigger the story. The sale of a company or a well-known brand, a substantial civil fine, a merger, a triple-platinum selling CD, a hugely successful play or book all generate news interest because of the money.

- *Hot investing trends:* During 2001 and 2002, when homeowners flocked to mortgage companies to refinance their homes, the media was filled with stories about real estate investing. If your company exemplifies a trend, then you're likely to find reporters who are receptive to your story.

- *General trends:* Patterns of three make a trend. If three entering Stanford University students happen to be the offspring of the rich and famous, you can count on seeing a story about how

Stanford is the hot college of the moment. When the success of CBS' *Survivor* spurred other networks to debut "reality shows," entertainment news enumerated them and covered the trend.

- *Scientific breakthroughs and disease cures:* It will be difficult to convince a reporter that your company is about to launch a product that is truly a bona fide scientific breakthrough or cure for a dreaded disease unless you have the proof—especially if the research is attached to a prestigious university or hospital. When AIDS patients began responding favorably to medications like AZT, journalists began producing stories that said AIDS was no longer a death sentence. More recently, when a government agency verified that two private companies had developed promising new cancer treatments, journalists produced stories that detailed those companies.

- *Annual stories:* Back-to-school season often results in a story or two about private companies that manage public schools or the office supply business. Christmas shopping season usually begets a story reviewing the past year in the retail business. The crush of people at the airport the day before Thanksgiving focuses reporters' attention on the travel industry. All of these stories are done every year and if, for example, you own an office supply company that is donating new clothes and school supplies to homeless kids, then you have a great chance of getting a reporter to listen to your pitch.

- *Quarterly results and annual reports:* If yours is a public company, you are required to issue quarterly earnings and annual reports, and the media is likely to pick up your release if they deem it to be newsworthy. If you introduce a new product within a few hours of your earnings report, the media is more likely to cover it because you have given them a news peg.

- *Second bananas:* When the underdog wins, reporters love it. Even if the underdog doesn't win, reporters love the drama of their struggle. In 2003, Funny Cide, the unlikely winner of two of thoroughbred racing's most coveted crowns, prompted reporters to write about the horse and the group that owned it precisely because Funny Cide was an unlikely winner. For years, the second-largest car rental company, Avis, capitalized on that truism with their advertising slogan, "We try harder." Reporters are always interested in the products and strategies the Number-Two company employs in trying to topple Number One. When Krispy Kreme opened a donut shop in Northern California that was across the street from an old-fashioned mom-and-pop donut store, a reporter went to do a story on the owners of the mom-and-pop store and their reaction to the competition. The owners used the opportunity to talk about the merits of their donuts instead of complaining about the competition. The result was a story that caused hundreds of customers to flock to the mom-and-pop shop to show their support.

- *Business stars:* There are many legendary figures in business that get media coverage no matter what. A few examples include Ted Turner, Bill Gates, Paul Allen, Steve Jobs, Carly Fiorina, Eli Broad, Donald Trump, Jack Welch, and Martha Stewart. If a legend is involved in your business, reporters want to know about it.

- *Corporate crimes:* Any new scrap of information about a news-making business crime, like the Enron bankruptcy, is going to generate interest among reporters. If your company is involved in any aspect of the misdeed—whether solving the crime, testifying at the trial, or managing the business as it regroups—expect reporters to take notice. Martha Stewart's defenders say that her alleged crimes are of lesser consequence that many other accused CEOs. But the fact that Martha Stewart's fame was so widespread—beyond the traditional business news boundaries—means that any accusations against her will invariably get bigger coverage.

- *Space and astronauts:* Space exploration and companies that enable it or that develop products based on what we have learned in space, are always intriguing to reporters and their audiences. In the 1980s, news organizations began to take space exploration for granted, then the Challenger space shuttle exploded and news organizations scrambled to cover the story. Twenty years later, we saw the same phenomenon in action when the Shuttle Columbia exploded and killed everyone aboard. The increase in intense coverage has continued because news organizations have been more vigilant about knowing how space travel works in order to figure out what went wrong.

- *Rich people's cheapness:* The majority of Americans worry about earning their rent and dream about winning the lottery. They think that if they had all that money, they would be generous and remember all the little people. When rich people are shown to be hoarders of hotel soaps, miserly tippers, or shoplifters, people want to read about it. It's been 20 years since hotel magnate Leona Helmsley said paying taxes was beneath her and only for the "little people." But people remember because to most of us, it is outrageous that a millionaire who had every comfort in life would be so cheap that they would seek to avoid paying taxes like the rest of us.

- *Powerful people's arrogance:* The sense of fair play that most Americans subscribe to includes the notion that we're all equal. When powerful business executives act like they are above the law and treat the less powerful with contempt, the press loves exposing that bad behavior. For example, Lizzie Grubman, a New York publicist who counted major celebrities among her clients and whose father is a rich and powerful attorney, had the media spotlight thrust on her after she called residents of a Long Island beach town "white trash," drove her Mercedes into a crowd in front of a local nightclub, and then fled the scene, ignoring the people she injured. Her major crime was her arrogance, which was noted in stories and headlines such as *Newsweek*, which carried a story under the headline, "Lizzie: Driving While Arrogant." Grubman served time in jail and she is still making headlines.

- *The first, last, biggest, smallest, youngest, oldest:* When you can legitimately apply any of these superlatives to a story, reporters' ears perk up. For example: the first movie star to earn $20 million a film; the last issue of a long-published magazine; the biggest civil fine ever imposed by a court against a company; the largest Initial Public Offering ever executed; the youngest CEO to head a major company; the oldest company in America changing its name.

- *Any story that features the mug shot of a celebrity:* It doesn't matter if the celebrity is merely the son or daughter of a well-known CEO, if he or she has been arrested, that police mug shot will result in stories.

- *Diets:* We're all looking for the magical chocolate bar that will make 10 or 20 pounds disappear. Most of us will try anything, as long as we don't have to actually eat less and exercise more. Companies with new diet products often generate media coverage.

- *Bad crimes in nice neighborhoods:* Fear is the element of drama that is at work in these stories. People will pay attention to a story about a carjacking in Detroit's most exclusive suburb or a home invasion robbery in Beverly Hills. Recently, a story about teenagers in an upper-middle class neighborhood trashing the home of a schoolmate whose family was on vacation prompted an avalanche of coverage.

- *Personal protection:* Crime rates have decreased overall across the United States, but peoples' fear of crime is forever on the rise. Anything that makes us feel safer in a world where children are kidnapped out of their front yards in broad daylight, is something media consumers want to know about.

- *Hollywood:* The inner workings of star-making machinery is fascinating and dramatic, featuring clashing egos, loads of money, and conflicts between images and reality. For example, when columnist Art Buchwald sued Paramount Pictures for taking something he wrote, turning it into the 1988 film *Coming to*

America, and denying him adequate payment, the ensuing stories about the strange financial practices at work in the movie business spawned headlines and books galore.

- *Hypocrisy:* Outspoken CEOs who are accused of lying on their resumes are prime targets for negative stories. A company that hires a celebrity to promote a product that they don't use in their real life also is a wide-open target. When the president of a prestigious college was discovered to have faked his academic credentials, the press was all over the story. Additionally, the marriage of Bill and Hillary Clinton receives a lot of ink because many reporters are skeptical of the couple's public face of togetherness.

- *Robots:* For decades, people have been envisioning the day when robots could take care of all the mundane tasks none of us want to do. Any company that has a product that that brings us closer to that is a natural story—for example, a remote-control vacuum cleaner that was unveiled in 2002 received a good deal of coverage.

- *People whose life stories have been turned into movies:* For example, everyone is now interested in anything that happens to Erin Brokovitch. When she announced that she was investigating a particular company for environmental pollution, it generated controversy and coverage.

- *The flavor of the moment:* It might be a song that everyone is humming or the commercial phrase that catches on. For example, the greeting made popular by hip-hop music, "Whassup" or its abbreviated version, "'Sup," made news when it crossed over into general usage. This also happens with business philosophies. A couple of years ago, when customer relationship management (CRM) was a major marketing trend, there were dozens of stories about companies that produced CRM software. The notoriety of recent accounting scandals, such as the Enron and Adelphia scandals, resulted in stories about companies that produce products that enable "transparency."

- *Dethronings:* When an idol is discovered to have feet of clay, it makes news. The first time Mike Tyson lost a boxing match or when Martha Stewart faced an insider trading investigation spawned headlines.

- *Disaster stories:* Natural disasters like earthquakes, airline crashes, tornados, and hurricanes provide dramatic backdrops for human interest stories. Manmade disasters like airline crashes and freeway pile-ups provide the same kind of drama. And drama makes stories.

- *Secret societies:* What really goes on within the inner sanctum of a company known for its secrecy? What is the secret to IBM's success? What did George W. Bush do when he was a member of Yale's exclusive Skull and Bones Club? Inquiring minds want to know.

- *President Clinton:* Love him or hate him, there is no doubt that people are interested in every move he makes. Anyone who worked for him and has now gone into business can expect reporters to follow his progress and his failings. Clinton is widely regarded to be a gifted leader whose tragic flaw led to unprecedented victories and defeats and any development within his life and business dealings makes news.

Stories That Are a Hard Sell

No story is impossible to get a reporter interested in, if only because the sheer size and breadth of today's media, with web sites, fanzines, and a plethora of trade magazines in every field. The trick is to find the right reporter for your story.

There are still stories that aren't front-page naturals, so you need to know what you are up against when you are pitching a tough story. Here are some examples of stories that, absent any of the distinguishing characteristics we just listed, will be a tough sell:

- *Disgruntled employees:* Reporters and editors take a skeptical view of former employees who rat on their ex-bosses because, usually, the ex-bosses paint the former employee as crazy and disgruntled. (Reporters themselves regularly fight with their editors and producers believing they could do a better job than their bosses.) Any former employee who seeks positive coverage regarding a grievance needs to be highly credible, to present the evidence in a believable manner, and to be ready to discredit their boss' rebuttal.

- *New product launches and grand openings:* Unless the product or the store has captured the nation's attention to the point where it has become a fad, then stories that center on new products for sale and new stores opening are too similar to an ad to interest many reporters. However, if the story is about the first inner city Wal-Mart or the most expensive Barbie doll ever, reporters will show up.

- *Most proposed legislation:* These stories often are too complex and slow moving to get much attention from the mainstream press. There is simply not enough time to report on all of them. An exception is legislation that is proposed in the immediate aftermath of a headline-making crime. For example, following the rash of kidnappings in the United States during the summer of 2002, many states inaugurated new laws against crimes on children and adopted the "Amber Alert" system. Those developments were widely covered in the news media.

- *Most press conferences:* Reporters don't have time to attend press conferences unless they are positive there will be significant news announced there. During the O. J. Simpson murder trial, for example, I received a notification for a press conference to announce that no-name actors dressed as cartoon characters would be making an appearance at a local movie theater. Clearly, I wasn't going to abandon the real story I was covering to attend this press conference.

- *Charitable events:* Reporters tend to roll their eyes when asked to cover pancake breakfasts, high school car washes, and Rotary Club speeches. Unless your event is extremely photogenic, such as a rally of 10,000 Harley motorcycle riders, or unless there is something extraordinary about your event, such as an A-list celebrity in attendance, then don't waste your time asking for major coverage. Instead, seek a mention in a column or a brief item in a calendar roundup.

- *Run-of-the-mill lawsuits:* Anyone can file a lawsuit. It's a legal judgment or jury verdict that makes a story.

- *Most new-hire announcements:* Unless you are a notable company announcing a new senior executive, most reporters will yawn and tell you to send your announcement to the part-timer who writes the business briefs column.

- *Other journalists:* Reporters rarely write stories about other journalists or even about other media companies. A reporter or a media company has to be involved in something huge for the media to write about it. A politician will be excoriated for playing a free round of golf, but a media company has to be the featured player in the scandal of the century to make the news. No, it's not fair. It's just the way it is.

These lists of stories that naturally make news and stories that are a hard sell are a good starting point to help you develop your sense of news judgment.

You can exercise your news judgment by reading newspapers and magazines and watching business TV shows, taking note of the stories that receive major coverage. If, for example, your company is in the water conservation business and your local newspaper is extensively covering drought conditions in your area, then coverage could be easy to obtain because the media is clearly interested in the issue.

KEY POINTS

It is natural that you are fascinated by your own business, but it is important to analyze how professional journalists see it. Develop your news judgment by looking at stories the way reporters do. It might be possible for you to find a new angle to your story that would make it more newsworthy.

HOMEWORK

➤ Take out the Alpha Dog Story idea you developed in Chapter 1. Using the lists in this chapter, analyze which newsworthy elements are found in your story idea. Does your story idea contain any of the "Not News" elements?

➤ Rewrite your Alpha Dog Story idea, inserting at least one of the news lures listed in this chapter.

➤ Analyze the front page of your local business section. How many stories fall into the natural stories list?

PART TWO

PRACTICE FACING THE MEDIA

Key Message Point Workshop

Lesson Plan

Key Message Points are your company's invaluable tool for getting through to reporters. In this chapter, we work on how to best formulate your company's Key Message Points and how to employ them when communicating both with the media and with your key audiences, such as your employees and customers. Sticking to your Key Message Points allows you to exert more control on the reporter's final story.

Now that you have a sense of what stories will interest the press, let's turn to other aspects of communicating with a journalist. After a reporter asks a question, he is not only listening to your answer but he is simultaneously formulating his next question, taking notes, and worrying about whether he'll meet his next deadline. Even when it is just you and a reporter in a room without any other apparent distractions, there are so many things competing for the journalist's attention that he can't give undivided attention to every word you say.

Instead, the reporter is listening for the themes that run through everything you say. He is listening for your major topics and arguments. He is listening for your *Key Message Points.*

Formulating your Key Message Points is the most important preparation you can do for your company, even more important than stocking your inventory or hiring the right staff. Think of it this way: If you cannot articulate what your business is, let alone how it is different or superior to your competitors, you won't be able to convince vendors to give you a price break and you won't be able to lure a top-notch staff in the first place. You certainly won't be able to make the most of an interview opportunity when it comes your way.

The way to formulate your Key Message Points is to make a list of facts about your company. Opinions don't matter here; only facts are allowed. Don't worry about putting them in any particular order because we'll learn how to organize them later. Just write as fast as you can.

Here's a checklist to help you compile all the facts:

- Describe your company in 10 words or less.
- What was last year's revenue?
- What are annual sales?
- What is the company growth by quarter or by year?
- What are dividends by quarter or by year?
- What is your target market?
- What is your secondary target market?
- Provide names and background of senior staff.
- When was the company founded?
- How many employees are there?

- How many clients do you have?
- How did the company begin?
- What is the size of the industry in which the company competes?
- What are the future goals for the company?
- Describe the various products or services the company offers.
- What is the number of products or services the company offers?
- What are your channels of distribution?

Once you have all your facts down, then you can start writing your Key Message Points.

Keep your list of Key Message Points short because the fewer points you have to make, the more control you have over the final media story and the more likely the story will reflect what you want to communicate. I recommend limiting your list to five Key Message Points.

Here is an example of why Key Message Points are essential. I was at the beach for the weekend with one of my friends, a major magazine editor, and his family. Late one afternoon, my friend's cell phone rang. It was a newspaper reporter wanting to interview him about a business development in an industry his magazine intensely covers. So my friend began talking and he kept on talking. I turned to my friend's wife and said, "He won't like the story when it comes out."

"Why?" she asked. "Isn't he explaining it enough?"

"He's explaining it too much," I said. "When she starts writing the story, she's going to have too much good stuff and she won't be able to make a decision about what to use. She's going to be overwhelmed."

Sure enough, the next morning, when we went on the Internet and found the story, my friend was dismayed.

"She didn't use my best stuff!" my friend said. "I sound boring and stupid."

"Sally called it. You should have listed to her," his wife said.

"How did you know?" my friend asked me.

I know simply because I was once a reporter. In any story, a reporter has room to make only a handful of points. To make matters worse in this particular case, the reporter who called my friend was clearly a beginning reporter because she didn't have enough seniority to get out of working the weekend. A beginning reporter will simply feel overwhelmed by too much information, which is what my friend gave her. As the reporter's deadline approached, she didn't have enough room for all of my friend's observations and she lacked the experience or sophistication to cram his best thoughts into a 750-word story. My friend's most insightful quotes ended up being left out. This won't happen to you if you keep a tight reign on your Key Message Points.

Keep Your Key Message Points Focused and Concise

One reason to keep your Key Message Points focused is because it keeps you within the lines of what you can and cannot say. For example, if your company is public, or if you are planning to go public at some point in the future, it is against the law for you to make certain statements that could be construed as hyping the value of the company or soliciting investors. If your company is small, then you certainly wouldn't want to broadcast your ideas for future growth, especially if your toughest competitor is conveniently located right down the street.

When it comes to going public with a company's business plans, I always advise clients to err on the side of caution. Once you have a first draft of your Key Message Points, send them to your lawyer for review. If your lawyer nixes one of the points, ask for a recommendation of how to get that point across in a way that would be legally acceptable. For example, most attorneys would delete any Key Message Point that states a company's plans for a merger, acquisition, or Initial Public Offering. However, the attorney would probably approve a Key Message Point that states that the company is committed to growth and doing the best it can for its investors.

Key Message Points are not static. When companies expand, alter their business model, enter new partnerships, or face any kind of new challenge, the Key Message Points should be rewritten.

As a general rule, initiate a Key Message Point workshop at least once a year. Call your senior team together in a conference room, follow the steps as listed next, and, within a few hours, you will have a new draft of your company's Key Message Points.

Once you have a list of all the facts about your company, go through the list and decide which facts are the major themes and which facts support those major themes. The major themes become your Key Message Points and the supportive facts become subpoints. Remember, you only get five Key Message Points, but there is no limit on the number of subpoints for each Key Message Point. You could have 100 subpoints, if you want. (Bear in mind, though, the more subpoints you have, the harder it will be to remember them when you're in the hot seat of an interview.)

Key Message Point #1 should be a general statement about your company:

"XYZ, Inc. is a leading developer, manufacturer, and supplier of widgets."

- Company XYZ focuses on selling a widget to fit every need and budget.

- Since Company XYZ was founded 10 years ago, the product line has expanded from one widget to 250 different widgets.
- Company XYZ markets its widgets under the ABC brand. Company XYZ also manufactures widgets that are sold under retail stores' private labels.

Key Message Point #2 should focus on the company's financial statistics:

"Company XYZ is in an aggressive growth phase."

- Company XYZ has shown tremendous growth between 1995 and today. Last year, our revenues were $700 million, compared to the previous year's revenues of $426 million.
- This year, the company is on track to meet a new goal of manufacturing and distributing more than 1 billion widgets.
- Company XYZ's earnings record is impressive.
  —1998, 5 cents a share
  —1999, 21 cents a share
  —2000, 52 cents a share
  —2001, 99 cents a share

Key Message Point #3 should focus on the company's target markets:

"Company XYZ makes a widget for men, women, and children of all ages."

- Company XYZ began with one widget. Today, Company XYZ makes more than 250 styles and sizes of widgets.
- Company XYZ makes or designs 60 percent of the world's widgets, including widgets marketed under leading retail chains' private labels.

---

*Key Message Point #4 should address
the company's future growth:*

*"Company XYZ is exporting its business
model internationally."*

- During the past three years, our overseas orders have doubled.
- We foresee much potential in overseas markets. Our goal is to have global markets account for as much as 25 percent of our sales within the next three years.
- Company XYZ has recently opened an office in Beijing and is currently looking to open two more offices and manufacturing facilities in Asia.
- We currently have 620 employees and plan to hire 300 additional employees in order to grow our global business.

---

*Key Message Point #5 can cover whatever
hasn't been covered in the other message points.*

*Point out what makes the company unique:
"Company XYZ sets the trends for widgets and our
customers receive the highest service in the industry."*

- Every employee at Company XYZ is required to submit one new idea for a new widget per quarter.
- One of the reasons we are so successful at making widgets is that our senior staff brings their extensive experience in the fashion, entertainment, and communications industries to the making of widgets.
- In a recent study by the University of Kalamazoo, which ranked widgets according to effectiveness and customer satisfaction, 12 of Company XYZ's widgets were listed in the top 15.
- The customer service department is staffed by experts who must pass a three-part exam and 65 hours of training. When

you call us, you don't get voice mail. You get a real live widget expert on the other end.

As you can see, these Key Message Points are concise and fact-based, and they give the listener an impressive overview of your company's strengths. Now that you have your Key Message Points written, you're ready for the next two chapters, which teach you communication mistakes to avoid and how to enact your Key Message Points.

KEY POINTS

Key Message Points are the themes you want to communicate about your company. They are not advertising slogans, but are based on the underlying facts of the company. The simpler the Key Messages, the more easily understood they will be to reporters and the public. Also, the simpler the Key Messages, the more naturally you will be able to employ them during interviews or when conversing with business associates.

HOMEWORK

➤ Compile the facts about your company and use them to write your Key Message Points. Show them to your lawyer as well.

➤ Convene a meeting with your company's officers and together, edit your company's Key Message Points.

➤ Pick a date six months from now and schedule a review of your company's Key Message Points during which time you may add and delete Key Message Points as needed.

CHAPTER

6

Lethal Mistakes: The Dirty Dozen

Lesson Plan

How you say something is as important as what you say. Before you commit yourself to content, learn how to deliver your message in a credible way. In this chapter, you learn how to avoid some of the most common mistakes businesspeople make during media interviews.

Before we work on *what* you are going to say during an interview, we first need to discuss *how* you are going to deliver your message. Here are some of the biggest mistakes to avoid. I call these mistakes *The Dirty Dozen:*

1. *Fudging, skirting the issue, spinning.* Whatever you want to call it, it's lying. When a reporter finds out you lied, he will extract justice. Stick to the facts. The term *spin* has

73

become very popular lately. But soon after it came into common usage, spin became a derogatory term for people trying to manipulate their media coverage. That isn't exactly the kind of media reputation you should be trying to build, especially because reporters resent it when they think you are trying to spin them.

2. *Winging it.* Just because you feel at home in a boardroom doesn't mean you're ready for prime time media. Matt Lauer is on television every morning, but he goes home every night with a pile of homework so he knows what he's talking about the next morning. Read your company's own public relations information, surf your web site, make a list of potential questions you might be asked—and don't go easy on yourself. Remember, reporters' queries usually have a "yes, but" context about them, as in, "Your company has been really successful to this point, but how can anyone sustain this level of success?" Or, "Your Company was ordered by the court to pay restitution of $10 million. Isn't that going to be a hardship?" The most important thing you can do is practice, practice, practice. Make a list of points you *want* to make and be ready to answer the questions quickly so you can segue to your list of points and say what you want to say.

3. *Thinking a reporter won't find out something you don't want him to know.* Don't ever lull yourself into thinking that the reporter likes you so much that he would never call your adversary to ask them about you. Of course, he is going to call the other side; that is the essence of a reporter's job. You have a right to expect fairness and maybe a chance to rebut any specific charges against you and your company.

4. *Giving just the facts, ma'am.* You can't expect an outsider to draw the same conclusions you do or to know what you know. When a reporter asks you a question, answer with a declarative statement, then lay out the facts and finish by putting those facts into your own context. I call it wrapping

your answer up in a big red bow. For example, during a recent interview with one of my clients, the CEO of a discount retail company, the reporter said, "During this recession, your sales can't be meeting your expectations." My client responded, "Quite the contrary. Our sales are 62 percent above our projections for this quarter precisely because of the recession. Our customers are looking for the best deals and when they shop with us, they get more for their money, so they are coming to us because of our price points and abandoning other retailers." My client put the facts into context for the reporter, and didn't leave it up to the reporter to speculate as to why my client's company could be succeeding during a down economy.

5. *Being too afraid to say, "I don't know."* An interview should be a conversation, not a test. It's fine to say on live television, "I don't know the exact number, but what I can tell you about our distribution network is. . . ." It's much better to admit you are unsure than to be a know-it-all for a minute.

6. *Failing to recognize that winning in the court of law and losing in the court of public opinion, is not a victory.* Just ask Gary Condit, who hasn't been charged, indicted, or convicted but has been ruined just the same. When you're involved in a legal proceeding or an investigation, or even if you're just under an umbrella of suspicion, you can't just let legal briefs or press releases speak for you; this is why O. J. Simpson "co-wrote" a book with Lawrence Schiller while he was in jail. The book didn't say anything substantive about the murders of his exwife or her friend. All it said, over and over again, was that O. J. was innocent and he would prove it later. Johnnie Cochran reinforced that message every time he strolled into court.

7. *Never using your company's name.* If you forget to refer to your company by name, then you risk having the people

who read or watch your interview think that the name of your company is "We" or "Us." Make sure you use your company name to build brand recognition.

8. *Waiting to return reporters' phone calls.* Reporters need to move fast, so you have to keep up with them. The minute they sell their editor or producer on doing a particular story, the clock starts ticking and the editor wants the story instantly. When reporters call, make sure someone calls them back immediately. If nothing else, it builds goodwill. Even if you can't help them with their story, if possible, give them the name and number of someone who can.

9. *Believing reporters are your friends.* Furthermore, don't act as if reporters are your enemies. The truth is somewhere in the middle and it's really very simple: Reporters are fun and interesting people, but they have a job to do. Their job is to be an observer and an interpreter. Treat them with respect— don't keep them waiting, offer them a cup of coffee—but don't expect anything more than fairness.

10. *Forgetting that everything leaks.* If anyone other than your lawyer knows, you can rest assured that the secret is making the rounds. It's a law of nature for which the *National Enquirer* is particularly grateful: People talk to each other about other people. This is where the Brother-in-Law Rule comes into play. That is, once 30 people know your secret, you should figure that at least one of the 30 has a brother-in-law who is a journalist.

Here is how to work around the fact that people talk: At the beginning of a business deal, plan your announcement strategy. When you complete the deal, make your announcements quickly so you retain more control. If your company is in the midst of a sensitive, but public, situation—whether it's as the defendant in a shareholder's lawsuit, a significant change in executive management, or a merger—expect that your decisions, conversations, and confidential documents will find their way to a reporter.

Memos and e-mails must be written sparingly and with care. Never put in writing anything you would not want to see on the front page. E-mails simply are too easy to forward to someone else, so take extra care when writing them.

11. *Losing control.* In journalism, as in life, the only thing you can control is your own behavior. It's easy to forget that you have more control than you think. The first order of business is to never wait for a reporter to give you an opening to talk about what you want to let the public know (including, of course, your investors, employees, and customers). Answer the question and segue to one of your Key Message Points.

    Generally, your answers—not the questions—are the most memorable parts of a broadcast interview and the only parts of a print story. Control the answers by being in control of your Key Message Points. Also remember that whenever you talk to a reporter, it is on the record and available for direct attribution. Many reporters don't believe there is any such thing as "off the record." Others think it means that they can use the information as long as they are vague as to the source (which probably could be traced to you, anyway). Finally, whenever you are around microphone, there is likelihood that you are being recorded. That's how George W. Bush was caught calling a *New York Times* reporter a foul euphemism.

12. *Saying "No comment."* People resort to saying "no comment" when they are under siege, caught off-guard, or scared of saying too much. There are some good reasons to fall back on "no comment," such as if you're being asked about your company's response to litigation and the lawyers have advised you to say nothing. However, as I explained in Chapter 2, once you say "no comment," you are perceived as having something to hide and therefore as guilty. Plus, there is nothing left to say because you've drawn the line in the sand

with your "no comment," thereby losing the opportunity to communicate your side of the story.

There are so many other things you can say without resorting to "no comment." One example: "You know, I can't address rumors but what I can tell you is that I think our company is on the right track. Our customers and our employees are really excited about our new product line. Once we reach the end of this project, I'd love to come back and update you." Another example: "I can't talk about the case because it is in front of the jury but I can say that I believe the truth will come out and that we will be exonerated."

Avoiding the mistakes listed here will help ensure that a reporter clearly hears your Key Message Points and that the resulting story will more accurately reflect your company's news.

KEY POINTS

➤ The number-one mistake people make when speaking to the media is saying, "No comment."

➤ Don't attempt to "spin" the truth; stick instead to fact-based statements.

➤ Saying something off-the-record is no guarantee it won't show up in the press.

HOMEWORK

➤ Come up with three new ways of saying "no comment" without using those particular words. Example: "I'd love to talk about the legal settlement, but unfortunately, our agreement stipulates that it remain confidential. But what I can tell you is that when we entered into the agreement, we had our shareholders' and our employees' best interests in mind."

Playing the Interview Game and Winning

Lesson Plan

An interview is a contest of control between an interviewer and an interviewee. You retain control by knowing the rules for using your Key Message Points to your advantage and by sticking to the facts. In this chapter, we see how to effectively employ Key Message Points to answer reporters' questions while controlling the interview. Memorization and defensiveness are sure-fire strategies for failure.

When instructing their clients about how to act during an interview, the technique many media trainers teach is that you should never listen to the question. Unfortunately, most media trainers haven't been journalists themselves, and they don't know how transparent and annoying that technique is to journalists. Moreover, if you've annoyed the reporter, it's safe to say that you haven't won the interview game—there's no need to look at the story that results from it.

Additionally, as our culture has become progressively media saturated, the public becomes more and more media savvy, to the point where today, those who employ the no-answer technique are widely perceived as less credible spin-meisters.

For example, flash back to the hotly anticipated and much-watched August 2001 interview Connie Chung conducted with Gary Condit, the California congressional representative in the middle of the Chandra Levy missing intern mystery. For more than 100 days, as vigilante-minded television pundits accused him of being an adulterous cad and a candidate for an obstruction of justice charge, Condit stayed quiet.

As the story swirled around him, Condit appeared arrogant, with his tight smiles and clichéd blow-dried politician hair. On the flip side, his constituents continued to defend him and polls showed they were sticking with him, calling him a caring man who had done much for his district. These conflicting images of Condit served to heighten the drama and increase the audience for his first television interview.

Everyone who tuned in to hear Condit finally defend his side of the story could tell he had been obviously scripted because he never answered any question. No matter what Chung asked, all Condit seemed to care about was repeating the same defensive talking points. The end result of the interview was that Condit came off sounding like an evasive, heartless opportunist. His answers did not fit the questions. Condit's gambit to increase his credibility and respectability ended up eroding it beyond repair.

By relying exclusively on scripted talking points, regardless of the questions asked of him, Condit did just about everything wrong. As a result, the camera recorded a man who appeared to have something to hide. He acted like he didn't owe an explanation for any aspect of his behavior, no matter how much he had betrayed the public trust. If Condit had only thrown away his script and spoken from his heart, the outcome might have been very different.

Talking points are fine and most of the time they are necessary. It is how they are used that creates the problems.

---

*When an interview subject's responses sound
like they were written by a public relations
professional, approved by a lawyer, and then memorized
verbatim, the interviewee loses all credibility. Furthermore,
an interview subject isn't really connecting with the
interviewer when the responses are too canned.*

As an alternative to the concept of talking points, try the *Organic Keyword Method*. Here is the guiding philosophy behind the Organic Keyword Method: Don't try to be perfect because you might succeed. Nobody likes a goody-goody who's got every nod of the head, every over-emphasized syllable down pat. More importantly, they don't believe his message. It is far preferable to be a real person who stutters a bit when he gets excited, or an executive who blushes when the interviewer gives him all the credit for the company's growth.

---

*During an interview, if you present yourself as confident,
sincere and a bit spontaneous, but not arrogant or rehearsed,
reporters will respect you and the public will listen to you.*

Preparing for Interview Success

To adequately prepare to succeed in an interview situation, you need to prepare to answer "Yes, but" questions. If you have the kind of public relations person on staff who asks only the gentlest of questions, then your Q&A sessions might feel good at the moment, but in the long run, I doubt you are getting good preparation or advice. If you have a public relations person who preps you with tough questions, you are on the right track for success.

In addition, when preparing, remember that it's the easy questions that often pose the biggest problems. For instance, many political experts believe that former President George Bush lost the presidential election to then-Arkasas Governor Bill Clinton when, during a debate, a journalist asked him the price of a loaf of bread. Although President Bush could expound on inflation rates and employment indices, he couldn't answer the question. Nobody prepped him for such an easy question.

Don't go overboard on preparation. Adequately preparing yourself does not equal memorization. Rather than attempting to memorize your Key Message Points, internalize them.

Know your Key Message Points so well that you can speak about your company without sounding like you are reciting a list. Don't try to say it exactly the same way every time. You should not bring a copy of your Key Message Points into an interview. Your goal is to appear as the epitome of confidence, but if you walk into an interview with canned responses, you'll come across poorly.

Relax on the Day before Your Interview

The day before a big interview, your first step should be to look over your Key Message Points and run through a few practice questions and answers. Your next step should be to relax. Go for a run, have a good meal, or listen to a favorite CD. If you enjoy what you do and feel relaxed, it will come across to a reporter and the audience.

Exercise prior to an interview and try to control your breathing during your time in the hot seat. Whenever I have a media opportunity, I center myself through practicing yoga. Here are some quick lessons on relaxation that I've learned.

Concentrate on Your Breathing

In yoga, you are taught specifically not to think. You concentrate on your breathing, which is not as easy as it sounds. By consciously trying to make your mind blank, you learn the importance of being fully present in the moment and not having your mind wander and your thoughts jump from one anxiety to another. As you prepare for your interview, try to relax and clear your mind by simply concentrating on your breathing.

Inhale normally, through your nose. Exhale also through your nose, but as you exhale, you place the back of your tongue on the roof of your mouth. The result is that you sound a little like you are breathing through a snorkel and diving mask.

Breathing is something we do naturally and most of us never give it a thought. Breathing deeply is something most of us don't do during the course of a normal day. But sometimes, when we find ourselves in stressful situations—such as an interview—we actually stop breathing. As a result, we're not getting enough oxygen and that makes us more anxious. It also affects our appearance. The reason photographers urge us to say "cheese" when they snap your photo is that it forces you to breathe. You photograph better when you don't look stiff and uncomfortable.

Remain Calm and Responsive

As you enter your interview, also remember to remain alert but calm. Do not lose your focus for even a millisecond. The minute you lose focus during an interview is the minute the reporter asks a question that throws you off.

Also in yoga, you learn to do something difficult while remaining calm and composed—equanimity. No matter what trying situation you may find yourself in, remember what my yoga teachers say: "Anybody can look calm when they are standing still. But remaining calm when you're falling is true equanimity."

Try taking that concept of equanimity into interview situations. Let's say you're asked a tough question, a question for which you are absolutely not prepared. If you show that the question has rattled your nerves, you can come off as being defensive, angry, or guilty of crimes you never even thought of. If you are asked a tough question and you remain calm, it makes it easier for you to bridge back to one of your Key Message Points and regain control.

Resist the Urge to Judge Yourself

Another point my yoga teachers stress is to refrain from judging yourself. If the teacher tells us to go into a pose where we are balancing on one foot, I might wobble and lose my balance. Instead of thinking to myself that I am no good at yoga, that I look ridiculous, my yoga teacher advises me not to waste time judging myself and, instead, concentrate on the pose. The same principle applies in interview situations, especially if you are on a live broadcast.

> *If you are trying to make your Key Message Points, but you are simultaneously judging yourself, then you're not going to sound confident or competent. You are going to start censoring yourself and making yourself nervous.*

The interview won't be successful for you or your business. And it certainly won't be successful for the interviewer, either, because a nervous interview subject generally doesn't provide a good interview.

Perhaps the biggest lesson yoga can teach a *Media Training 101* student is humility, because, just like yoga, an interview is continuously challenging, no matter how many interviews you have given. Just when you think you have it down pat is the moment a zinger comes flying right at you. Practice and you will be able to remain calm and composed, no matter what happens. Just remember to breathe.

Trust Yourself during the Interview

I once had a client who just couldn't trust himself when it came to his Key Message Points. This client helped to invent a revolutionary treatment for a common ailment. It was easy for me to book him on a business television show to talk about his breakthrough, but the minute I booked the appearance, this easy-going, chatty, funny, likeable guy turned into a bundle of raw nerves. He insisted on doing practice sessions every day of the week leading up to his interview. He insisted on memorizing his Key Message Points. During practice sessions, he would berate himself if his answers didn't conform exactly to the script in his head. I saw disaster looming.

I told him that memorization was not the key to succeeding at his interview. I told him that he should, of course, know his Key Message Points, but not to the extent that his answers sounded canned. Finally, I told him that when he drove himself to his interview, instead of reviewing his Key Message Points at every red light, he should instead put on some good music and sing along at the top of his lungs.

My client didn't listen, no matter how forcefully I tried to guide him. He persisted in his memorization. By the time he went on the air, he was so worked up, it was clear to anyone who saw the interview that he was a nervous wreck. He was so nervous that he forgot to make some of the most important points about his product. All of the pressure he put on himself to memorize everything went to waste, and his product didn't get the bump in sales it could have garnered from such an opportunity.

My client got into trouble because he wanted to present himself as perfect instead of human. Don't fall for that; be natural. Remember that it is the unexpected that often makes life fun.

All the people you're trying to communicate to are human themselves and they identify with, believe in, and invest credibility in other humans—not in drones.

Be Prepared for Dramatic Questions

While you want to appear natural during an interview, you shouldn't adopt an excessively easy-going attitude. That's another clear path to big trouble because the most important ingredient in any journalism story is drama. Many, if not most, reporters ask their questions in a fashion designed to heighten the story's drama. That is also why reporters often joke with each other about asking the classic, drama-laden question, "When did you stop beating your wife?"

Why would a reporter ask a bland question such as, "What are the benefits of your product?" There is much more drama in a question like, "Why would anybody believe there are any benefits to your product?" However, without the benefit of media training, many business executives would visibly bristle at being asked such an impertinent question in an undoubtedly negative tone of voice. Their answer would, most likely, come off as defensive. "Why wouldn't our customers believe us?" an executive might respond. "We stand behind our products. I can't believe you would ask such a question. Is this what you call journalism?"

The journalist wins in such a situation because the executive has lost his temper and, as a result, the story has just gotten more dramatic.

No one who reads or watches the story will ever know that the journalist stacked the deck by intentionally asking an obnoxious question. In the editing process, the questions are left out. What is left in are your answers.

Executives are accustomed to being asked questions in a gentle and solicitous manner by the people who work for them. Journalists, however, take pride in asking tough questions of executives who are used to white-glove treatment. An executive who is aware that journalists inject a healthy dose of skepticism and cynicism into any question as a way of heightening their story's drama, would be prepared. Rather than react defensively, the executive would know not to take any question as a personal affront; the executive would recognize that the reporter is merely trying to heighten the story's drama. Remember, a story without drama is a story that won't make it into the news.

Let's look at the same scenario, but with a nondefensive response: The journalist asks, "Why would anybody believe there are any benefits to your product?"

The executive responds: "That's a great question, Dennis, and I guess I would tell our customers not to take my word for it. The University of Kalamazoo recently did a study on widgets and ranked them according to effectiveness. Twelve of our widgets made it into the top 15. In addition, we're also really proud of our customer service department, which is staffed by experts who must pass a three-part exam and 65 hours of training. When you call us, you don't get voice mail. You get a real live widget expert on the other end. So we aren't asking our customers to just blindly believe what we say. We want our customers to look at our actions, look at our record."

Clearly, this thoughtful response would make the company look appealing to the audience reading this article. Because the executive was able to control himself, he won at the interview game.

Avoid Appearing Defensive

Some executives can appear defensive simply because they have invested so much of themselves into building a successful company or career. It's a natural response because they want to protect their investors and employees, but when defensiveness shows up in an interview, the audience doesn't try to figure out the executive's motivation. The executive generally ends up appearing arrogant.

It is especially important to curb defensiveness when the interview is aired on radio and television. These days, talk shows are all about the hosts, not about the guests and not about the news. Shows like the *O'Reilly Factor* and the *Rush Limbaugh Show* might educate some people here and there about a relevant issue, but the education factor is often incidental. These shows are really forums for entertainment, and this flows from the host's persona and slate of underlying beliefs and principles. The only way guests are important is when the hosts use the guest in a short segment to spar with the host or to underscore one of the host's beliefs.

O'Reilly, for example, has made a name for himself by espousing an antiphony philosophy. That philosophy provides the fuel for O'Reilly to rail against government officials who, in his judgment, are soft on prisoners. O'Reilly believes prisoners shouldn't have any form of recreation because they should be miserable in prison so that they can think about their crime 24/7. O'Reilly also disparages other television interviewers like Connie Chung and Larry King because of his underlying belief that most of the media are spoon-fed their stories and don't have the guts to ask tough questions. He also regularly takes on corporate leaders for what he deems to be irresponsible behavior that in his estimation "hurts America," like when companies hire gangsta rappers to promote their products.

No matter who you are, you are not going to change his underlying beliefs. If you were to appear as a guest on O'Reilly's show, you would need to be aware that you will probably be put on the defensive. To his credit, O'Reilly respects any guest who holds an opposing viewpoint and who doesn't get rattled or rude when he aggressively questions that viewpoint. If you agree to appear on O'Reilly's program or another show to promote your belief that prisons should provide rehabilitation as well as punishment, then the best way to present your argument is not to argue with him. O'Reilly is probably always going to believe that prison inmates' main activity should be contemplating their past bad deeds. It would be much more effective for you to say something along the lines of, "Well, Bill, I know we have different opinions on this and I respect your belief. But after working for 20 years in the criminal justice system, I truly believe that when people are in prison, we need to teach them a better way to live because of the following facts."

Stand Your Ground but Remain Nondefensive

The minute you go on the defensive, you lose control, the reporter wins and you lose the opportunity to use his forum as a way to get your ideas into the national debate. However, being nondefensive

doesn't mean being a wimp. You need to present yourself as confident in your facts and not intimidated by the power of a reporter like
O'Reilly or by the fact that you are in the hot seat at the moment.

If the reporter makes a factual error in his question,
point it out before you launch into your answer.

When I conduct a media training session, during practice interviews, when I play the reporter, I often purposely call the executive I am training by the wrong name. I want to see if they can stay
focused and calm and yet set the record straight. "Interesting question, Sally, and I just want to let you know my name is James, before
I tell you that. . . ."

Notice how the error was not repeated when James corrected
the interviewer. He didn't say, "My name is James, not John." He
didn't make a big deal of it. But he didn't let it go, either.

It's important to point out the mistakes in a question. It doesn't
make as much difference when the fact that is in dispute is a name,
and not the amount of revenue a company brings in, but you still
have to learn how to correct a reporter's facts nondefensively. Even-
tually, a reporter will ask a question that contains a factual error of
significant consequences and you need to know how to handle that
situation gracefully and get the interview back on track.

Never Let Your Guard Down with a Reporter

With a little practice and solid, fact-based Key Message Points, you
will actually enjoy the interview process, even when you have a
tough, no-holds-barred interviewer like O'Reilly. However, no matter
how prepared you are, never relax too much when a reporter is
around. For example, one of my clients is a charming, handsome,
thirty-something entrepreneur who made a lot of money in the dot-
com craze. He came to me for help a few weeks after a major national
newspaper published a story on him concluding he was nothing but

a slick operator who lied on his resume and built companies that he sold at high valuations. Shortly after taking his profits, though, the companies he built floundered.

The story clearly portrayed him as an opportunist and a name-dropper. The most positive quote from one of his associates said he had an "evangelical style." Another said he was successful because he "didn't have to worry about the bottom line." The story also noted his Bel Air address, his Ferrari, and the fact that he had not yet invested in his new company because he was "not very liquid right now."

Through our discussions, I was able to analyze the many points at which the interview had gone wrong, but the main contributing factor was that the client had been media trained a bit too well. He was slick. He had a talking point for everything. He was a little too confident. Add to that lethal combination the fact that he was barely 30 and a little too good-looking. He'd been a little too successful at the dot-com game when many others lost too much money. Finally, to top it all off, his responses to questions sounded like he was reciting a script, and he talked too much, telling a reporter personal information about his fancy house and car and personal liquidity.

During our media training session, he became frustrated at my instructions to remain focused on the fact that he was in an interview, not at a social event. I repeatedly instructed him to answer the question and then shut his mouth—not blabber on about personal matters. Answer the question and then stop talking. However, once the first story was published and the depiction of him and his business was more accurate, he had to admit the Organic Keyword Method was working.

Remember the Ground Rules for Working with Reporters

Here is a quick review of four essential ground rules, before we discuss the way the Organic Keyword Method works:

1. Return phone calls promptly.
2. Provide the background a reporter needs.
3. Never, ever lie.
4. Don't be afraid to say, "I don't know."

1. *Return phone calls promptly.* A reporter is always at the mercy of a phone message. He gets an assignment and he then gets a deadline. Missing a deadline is not only out of the question, it often is a fireable offense. As we have discussed, when a source returns a reporter's call promptly, the reporter's anxiety level decreases.

You can always return the phone call; tell the reporter that you're in the middle of something and you can't talk long, but you wanted to make sure he knew you got the message. The reporter then will fill you in on his story idea and you can promise to call back in a few minutes. You have just bought yourself some time. Think about what you want to say and how it relates to your business and build your Key Message Points.

2. *Provide the background a reporter needs.* One of the simplest things that you can do to ensure a successful story is to make the reporter's job a little easier. For instance, if you have a good photo of an executive, offer to e-mail the reporter a copy of the photo—and then do it within the next hour. If you are seeking to be interviewed about a national effort—let's say it's a rollout of a program designed to inspire children to become more physically active—then put together a chart that gives the names of participating cities and towns and the events scheduled there and offer it in e-mail format to reporters. If you want a reporter to include your latest book or movie in their next entertainment roundup, make sure to send him a copy. If the reporter wants some suggestions about other people to interview about you, give him a positive contact's name and number.

3. *Never, ever lie.* We went over this in Chapter 1 when we discussed the Foundational Rules for Public Relations Success. But this rule against lying is so important it bears repeating.

It's not a moral judgment; it's a practical one. You'll get caught. After interviewing a few thousand other people, reporters have built in BS-detectors, for one thing. For another, you are not the only person a reporter will talk to on any given story. If what you say doesn't ring true, you would be lucky if the reporter cuts you out of the story, because otherwise, he will, most likely, expose you as a fraud.

Speaking of frauds, don't try to be something you're not. One of my clients, the president of a company with a very hot brand, is the kind of man who speaks cautiously—so cautiously, in fact, that a reporter for a major business magazine once said to me, "You don't have anything to worry about with Mr. X. He's so careful, he won't tell me anything you don't want him to say."

I replied, "You are seeing the real Mr. X. You have spent three days interviewing him. Believe me, he is just being who he is. He couldn't sustain a charade for that long."

The reporter nodded, knowing I had spoken the truth.

4. *Don't be afraid to say, "I don't know."* Remember, speaking the truth does not mean you have to know everything. Instead, simply say, "I don't know the answer to that but let me write it down and I'll get the answer and get back to you."

Laurie Levenson, the widely quoted associate dean of Loyola Law School and legal commentator, is a master at getting back to reporters. She's a teacher by temperament and by profession, so it's very natural for her to be helpful. Reporters call her all the time for her take on various legal goings-on and if a reporter hits a question that has a complex or unclear answer, Laurie will tell the reporter that she'll need to call back. And she will. Sometimes, the reporter will ask an obscure question that she knows will never make it into the story—just something she's curious about. She might then say not to bother. Three days later, Laurie will call her and tell her she went to two different law libraries and she'll fax her the precedent-setting case law. No wonder reporters call her back.

In many instances, the true sign of giving a good interview comes weeks later when the reporter calls back for another interview on a different story.

Now that we have the philosophy and the ground rules behind giving an interview, we turn in the next chapter to using the Organic Keyword Method. As we have discussed, most interviews are a contest of control between the interviewer and the interviewee. Remember what we have already gone over: You cannot control the reporter in any way. You cannot control the questions the reporter asks or his tone of voice when he asks the questions. That's the nature of news—it is random and unexpected. Your ability to portray yourself and your company in a positive way is in direct proportion to how adeptly you can answer the question and then immediately put your own message out there with the help of the Organic Keyword Method.

KEY POINTS

➤ Over-rehearsing is a recipe for failure because your responses appear canned and insincere. However, you should also never let your guard down whenever a reporter is around.

➤ Remember that reporters' questions often reflect a "yes, but" attitude and are geared toward eliciting drama from the interviewee.

➤ Remain nondefensive if a reporter asks you a potentially emotional or contentious question.

➤ If the reporter makes a factual error, don't be afraid to correct him before you answer with a Key Message Point.

HOMEWORK

➤ Videotape three different newsmakers being interviewed on three different television interview programs. Watch the videotapes with a critical eye, analyzing the interviewee's credibility, on-camera mannerisms, and effectiveness in delivering their message.

Putting the Organic Keyword Method to Work

Lesson Plan

In this chapter, we'll explain the Organic Keyword Method that enables you to answer any question, no matter how tough. You need to have your Key Message Points nearby as you learn the basics of employing the Organic Keyword Method. We also discuss the ABC Formula, which helps you use your Key Message Points in interviews.

If you are familiar with America Online (AOL), then you already know what a keyword is. For the rest of you, it works like this: You want to look up some online brokerages so that you can buy stock. On your AOL screen, click on the "keyword" button, then type in "stock" and click "Go." You are immediately taken to a page that gives you dozens of choices of web sites about stocks and personal finance.

We use that same principle in the Organic Keyword Method. The reporter asks you a question, you take a few seconds to breathe, and you begin answering the question that was put to you. While you are taking a breath, your brain has identified a *keyword* in the reporter's question that enables you to recall one of your Key Message Points. You segue to this Key Message Point and conclude your answer. The formula is as easy to remember as ABC:

- **A**nswer the question.
- **B**ridge to one of your Key Message Points and lay out the facts.
- **C**onclude by telling your interviewer what those facts mean.

For example, a reporter might ask the CEO of Company XYZ Widgets, "Doesn't the world have enough widgets?" Using the ABC formula, the CEO could begin his answer by saying, "Actually we believe the world needs more widgets." The CEO has already identified a keyword in the question. In this case, it is *world,* which leads the CEO to his Key Message Point about global expansion. He continues his answer by saying, "We foresee a lot of growth in over-seas markets because during the past three years, our overseas orders have increased by 200 percent. To take advantage of that op-portunity, we recently opened an office in Beijing and right now, we are planning to open two more offices and factories in Asia. Our goal is to have our global business account for as much as 25 percent of our sales within the next three years and we are planning to hire an additional 300 employees to service that market. We're delighted about our worldwide growth and we're going to do every-thing in our power to make Company XYZ the world's leading widget maker."

This answer was nice and neat. It was easy for the CEO to bridge to one of his Key Message Points.

Keep in mind that there is no "right" or "wrong" keyword in a journalist's question. In the example above, the executive keyed in on "world." He could also have keyed in on "widgets" and used it as a springboard to talking about the new developments.

Obviously, from time to time, a reporter will ask you a question you simply don't know the answer to or you haven't given it enough thought to answer. In those instances, it is best to use the ABC formula in the following way:

- **A**nswer the question by saying, "You know, I don't know the answer to that. I am going to have to give that some thought and get back to you."
- **B**ridge by saying, "But your question reminds me that when we started in this business, our product line consisted of one widget. Today, we make more than 250 styles and sizes of widgets."
- **C**onclude by saying, "And we aren't stopping with 250 widgets. We are constantly looking for new and better widgets so that we remain the leader in the widget industry."

Reliable bridging phrases include:

- What's important to remember is . . .
- I am not allowed to comment on pending litigation, but what I can tell you . . .
- Before we move on to another subject, I want to add . . .
- Even more importantly . . .
- You should also remember . . .
- There is more to the story, specifically . . .
- What I want to make sure you understand here is . . .
- You make a good point there, but our main consideration was . . .
- That reminds me . . .

Master Your Conclusion

When you are a beginner at the interview game, bridging to your Key Message Points is the most difficult aspect to learn and feel confident about using. In actuality, the part that is the toughest to master is the Conclusion. In some cases, the difficulty springs from when we were children and we were taught—and taught and taught—not to brag. In other cases, it is because the interviewee is so convinced that his beliefs are correct that he thinks anyone else who listens to the same facts will reach the same conclusion.

On the contrary, reporters, in general, are not creatures of subtlety, and an interview is not an opportunity for a reporter to become your mouthpiece.

The reporter is supposed to be objective, so if you want the readers or viewers to reach a certain conclusion, don't leave it to the reporter. The conclusion is the most important part of what you have to say.

Some phrases to help you ease into your Conclusion include:

- That is why we believe . . .
- When we look at all those facts that I just laid out for you . . .
- We are going to keep doing exactly what has brought us our success . . .
- As I said . . .
- What that means is . . .
- And that is the best part about . . .
- The important point here is . . .

When it comes to the conclusion, I coach my clients to "wrap it all up in a big red ribbon." In other words:

1. Answer the question.
2. Identify the keyword that allows you to bridge to your Key Message Point.
3. Lay out the facts that are the subpoints.
4. Make sense of the facts by wrapping them up and drawing a logical conclusion.

Use Every Opportunity to Reinforce Your Message

When I was a reporter, working mostly in newspapers, I always ended each interview the same way. As the interview was winding to an end, I would always ask, "Is there anything I didn't ask you about that you think is important for my readers to know?"

More often than not, the answer would be, "No, I think you got it all."

Now that I'm not a reporter anymore, I can tell you that that answer is unacceptable. Whenever a reporter signals that the interview is ending by asking a question like, "Anything else you want to say?" grab the opportunity to reemphasize your main point. It doesn't matter if you sound a little repetitive. This is the last chance you have to put something in the reporter's mind that will influence the writing or editing of the story.

If the interview is about anything the least bit controversial, calmly tell the reporter that you would appreciate the opportunity to respond if they are going to subsequently interview the other side. (Don't worry about putting the idea into the reporter's head. Whether you ask or not, it is a reporter's job to get all the sides to the story.) In the end, it is quite possible that you could choose not to respond, but at least you will be forewarned and you can figure out what the story will say before it hits the public.

In broadcast, there also is a signal for the end of an interview. You have heard it a million times. The interview is moving along and suddenly, the anchor says, "In our last 20 seconds, I want to ask you . . ." Whenever you hear any phrase like that, you can quickly answer the question and then immediately bridge to the most important thing you want the audience to remember about your interview. It might be an invitation to sign your petition on your web site, it might be that your movie opens on Friday, or it might be that your company set a sales record; whatever it is, don't hold back. The anchor has already signaled that there won't be a follow-up question so keep on talking your Key Message Points until you simply run out of air.

KEY POINTS

The formula that enables you to answer any question is ABC: Answer, Bridge, Conclude. The formula works in conjunction with your Key Message Points, enabling you to answer any question. When an interviewer indicates this is his last question, make the most of your final seconds and communicate your main message once again. Don't leave it to the reporter to infer your main points, and take advantage of every opportunity to segue back to your Key Message Points.

HOMEWORK

➤ For an entire day, answer any question put to you by employing your Key Message Points and the ABC formula. It might feel a bit awkward at first, especially when responding to a neighbor's polite query about the weather, but by the end of this homework assignment, you will be able to segue from talking about the weather to outlining your product's best qualities.

CHAPTER

9

Key Message Point Practice Questions

Lesson Plan

Now that you have your Key Message Points and you have learned how to use them during interviews, it's time to take a look at the kinds of questions that go into an interview. The best preparation for any interview is to review a list of questions. Remember, reporters rarely think any question is too personal or too pointed. This chapter helps you think of tough questions for your practice sessions.

What kinds of questions should you expect from a reporter? The truth is you can expect the unexpected. A reporter is not afraid to ask anything, and there is no such thing as a question too pointed, too personal, or too aggressive.

As you read down the list, you'll notice that I jump from one subject to the other without rhyme or reason. That is the way a real interview is. Consciously or not, reporters jump from one subject to another to gain an advantage over the interviewee. This is part of the tug-of-war over control of an interview.

You, on the other hand, have a great advantage if you have done your homework. You have developed and internalized your Key Message Points. You can handle each question, each twist and turn, because you know your core messages and have a firm plan of what you want to say publicly. You can take each question and use it as an opportunity to communicate your goals and vision, and you won't be rattled by a "Yes, but" reporter.

Before we launch into the list of questions, it is important to note that most questions fall into one of several categories:

- *Personal:* If a reporter asks you for intimate, personal details, answer briefly, without elaborating and then bridge to a Key Message Point. For example, a reporter might ask you the ages of your children. You could answer, "My kids are in grade school and helping them do their homework gave me the idea to start this company because . . ."

- *Controversial:* A reporter might ask you about your being fired from a previous position, or about a lawsuit that your company is facing. Remember to not lie; instead you might say, "I would love to tell you all about that, but unfortunately, I am not allowed to talk about it, other than to say that . . ." Remind the reporter about your present and future successes, and use this opportunity to emphasize the positive aspects of what your company is doing right now.

- *Repetitive:* As we have discussed, often a reporter asks the same question in many different ways. Many reporters preface repetitive questions by saying that they are not sure they understand your previously made point. (Often, however, reporters aren't confused; they are simply trying to uncover discrepancies so they can then ask you about them.) Don't show your frustration in this situation. Calmly re-explain your answer, focusing on your Key Message Points.

- *Technical:* Some reporters consider themselves an expert on the beats they cover. For example, a reporter who has covered the computer software company for years might ask an overly technical question in order to retain control of the interview, or to show off his knowledge. Regardless of the question, don't get too technical in your answer. Keep your answers short and simple enough for the average reader or viewer to understand your major points.

- *Hard-core business:* Many business reporters will focus several questions on business decisions that you might not have made yet. For example, an owner of a successful retail store could be asked about developing a chain of stores, or the CEO of a new computer company could be asked about his plans for an Initial Public Offering. Remember to not reveal anything you would not want to see on the front page the following day.

- *News events:* If your interview is taking place on the day after a major national news event, you could be asked for your opinion. It's fine to give your opinion as long as it won't offend your clientele and affect your business. Otherwise, I recommend that you say something like, "I haven't had time to formulate my opinion on such a complex subject," and quickly bridge back to a Key Message Point.

Sample Interview Questions

As mentioned earlier, the questions are mixed up so that each differs, both in style and substance, from the previous question. Don't let that throw you off. As long as you have internalized your Key Message Points, you will be able to go with the flow of the interview.

Here is a list of sample interview questions:

- What is your company's major product?
- What is your most profitable division?
- What makes you think that your company will succeed?

- I have heard that your company has this problem on the horizon. What do you have to say about that?
- How did you get the idea for this?
- What are your revenues?
- Have you ever been sued?
- A lot of people say that your company/product is too trendy to achieve long-term success. What do you say to that?
- Who are your core customers?
- Who or what is your major competition?
- I heard you were fired from your last job. Is that true?
- What are your primary obstacles in growing this company?
- You have been accused of _____. What do you have to say to that?
- How many employees do you have?
- I understand that you used to work in the _____ industry. How did you make the switch to this industry?
- What sets you apart from the competition?
- Why did you start this company?
- This particular employee of yours is really controversial. Why did you hire her/him?
- Your last company was accused of expanding too quickly. Aren't you making that same mistake again here?
- What is your most important product?
- Why do you say that? (Or, What do you mean?)
- What is new about your company?
- Why did this particular employee leave the company?
- You just sold a lot of stock at a delicate time for your company. Why?
- I heard there are going to be layoffs. Can you set the record straight on that?
- What is next for your company?

- In our last 30 seconds, can you explain _____ ?
- How many different products do you have?
- How do you spend your money?
- Your success has become a legend; but how can you keep up the success of this company?
- What interested you in starting this business?
- What is your background?
- How much money do you make?
- Your last product didn't meet its sales expectations. Why do you think it failed?
- A lot of people wouldn't think that your background would prepare you for this kind of company. What do you have to say to that?
- Do any of your relatives work for the company?
- What is your secret to success?
- Why aren't your products made in America?
- How old are you?
- Your ex-spouse is suing you. What is that all about?
- Don't you think people deserve to know?
- The City Council/Planning Commission just turned down your plans to build a new headquarters. What are you going to do about it?
- What is your personal life like?
- How will the current recession/economic slowdown affect your business?
- What is your company's growth strategy?
- How much profit do you make from each sale/transaction?
- Your last business went bankrupt. What makes you so sure that this one will succeed?
- I heard you just bought a new house/fancy car. Do you really think it's smart to spend like that in this economy?

- Your company was a big mess a couple of years ago. Revenues were down 75 percent and you were sued by a number of people. Why should anybody believe that things are different now?

- Do you have any patents?

- Who is your biggest enemy?

- I heard that you criticized the government's policy on business. Can you confirm this?

- Sure, you are growing, but isn't your profit margin shrinking?

- I heard that the government is investigating your company. Can you confirm or deny that?

- Can't you just answer that with a yes or no?

- Do you think the press has treated you fairly?

- What types of deals do you have coming up?

- Why are sales/revenues going up?

- Are you selling your company?

- What happens if you lose one of your big customers?

- Are you planning to open a new division?

- What makes you think your growth is sustainable over the long term?

- I heard you have tapped _____ to be your successor. But I hear that there has been a lot of internal turmoil about that selection. What do you have to say about that?

- Why did you donate to this political candidate? Isn't that just a bribe?

- Aren't you worried you're going to oversaturate the market?

- What is your biggest vice?

- Why are sales/revenues going down?

- Why don't people think your company can succeed?

- The governor just announced his new business plan. A lot of people are saying it's too expensive and we should put the taxpayers' money into education instead. What do you think?

- Isn't it just a matter of time before your product loses its cachet with the public? Then what will you do?

- A lot of people say that you are hard to get along with, that you are stubborn, and don't listen to your employees. What do you have to say to that? Why do people say that?

- Who inspects your factories?

- When will you retire?

The best way to practice with this list of questions is to write each question on a slip of paper, put the slips into a basket and pull them out one by one. Answer them. With this method, you will be able to approximate the random order in which many reporters ask questions. When you are driving and listening to talk radio, turn down the volume whenever you hear a question and try to answer the question yourself, using your Key Message Points.

Preparation and a solid set of Key Message Points is all you really need to ace your next interview.

KEY POINTS

➤ Remember, no reporter writes a story that includes a list of the questions they asked the interviewee. It's your answers that matter because that is what gets into the story.

➤ You can answer anything because you know what you want to say. Don't memorize your answers or your Key Message Points. Your goal is to appear fresh and spontaneous for each interview, not rehearsed.

➤ Many difficult questions fall into the following categories: Personal, Controversial, Repetitive, Technical, Hard Core Business, and News Events. The formula for answering difficult questions remains the same: ABC (Answer, Bridge, Conclude).

HOMEWORK

➤ Write at least 20 questions about your business. In formulating your questions, make sure that you employ the same "yes, but" attitude that a reporter would. Once you have your list of questions, practice, practice, practice circling back to your Key Message Points. Try answering each question at least two different ways.

➤ Role-play. Give a list of questions to a trusted colleague and have them play the role of reporter. Then switch roles. You be the reporter. Get into the mind-set of a reporter. What would a reporter ask if she knew everything about your business that you know? Listen to your colleague's answers when your colleague is playing your role. His answers might spark a good idea for you.

➤ Videotape yourself playing both roles. Review the tapes and critique your performance.

PART THREE

GIVING A
GREAT INTERVIEW

Interviews: What Is What and Who Is Who

Lesson Plan

Different kinds of interviews call for different strategies. If you're not prepared, different interview styles can throw you. Get ready for your interview by knowing what to expect in any media situation. In this chapter, we discuss strategies for preparing yourself for interviewing in any context.

Good interviews are not an accident. They might look effortless, but people who consistently give strong interviews know that before you sit down for any interview, you have to do your homework. Here are the steps to take for ensuring that your interview is stellar:

1. *Study up on your interviewer.* If you have never seen the show you have agreed to be a guest on, then you need to order and watch a few videotapes of the program. If you are being interviewed by a local newspaper reporter, look through back issues or go to the library to find other stories by that reporter so you can get a feel for his or her writing style. (This will also give you something to make small talk about before the interview begins.)

2. *Review your Key Message Points.* In addition, do some research to bolster your argument. For example, using statistics and facts will enhance your credibility and contextualize your Key Message Points. Make sure you anticipate both tough and easy questions, double-check any facts you intend to use.

3. *Have a sense of what type of story this is going to be.* When you agree to the interview, you should have a pretty good idea about the story the reporter is working on. In other words, is it a feature story that focuses only on your company? Are you just one of many people to be interviewed about a specific news event?

4. *Warm yourself up, and project energy.* Before the interview begins, take a moment to prepare your voice by clearing your

---

Most of all, approach each interview or public appearance with a certain mind-set:

- Acknowledge that you are an authority in your area of expertise.
- Demonstrate that you really care about your business and this interview.
- Say that you are glad to have the opportunity to speak directly to the reporter's readers or viewers.
- Even if you are not thrilled at being in the public eye, at least you can express thanks for the opportunity to set the record straight.

throat or warming up your vocal cords. When the interview begins, take an active role. Get your messages out there. If the reporter doesn't ask you the specific question you would like to answer, find an opportunity to say what you want to say. If appropriate, have photos or a chart to give the reporter for background.

Prepare Yourself for Interviewing in All Possible Settings

Among the other things you should consider, there's also the question of where the interview will take place. If the reporter gives you a choice on where you can conduct the interview, pick a setting that feels right to you. Most of the time, the setting is determined by the type of interview (broadcast or print; live or taped) or the amount of time the reporter has to work on a story (phone interviews are better for tight deadlines).

Every interview is different and the differences start with the setting. Here is what to expect in each type of interview.

Phoner

In the old days, reporters used to try to do all their interviews in person. However, as the cost of transportation rose and the news cycle got shorter and shorter, reporters resorted more and more to the telephone.

When doing a phoner, place the call on time and dial it yourself so that you don't appear to be so self-important that you don't place your own calls. It is perfectly acceptable to have your public relations person listening in on the call as long as you inform the reporter at the outset of the call.

Sound quality is of utmost importance; don't use a speakerphone or a phone of poor quality.

For *radio interviews,* speakerphones, cell phones, and cordless phones are no-nos. You don't want people to have to work hard to listen to your message.

When the radio host thanks you and says goodbye, thank him for the opportunity to be on his show and do not hang up for at least five seconds. If you plunk down the phone right away, there will be an audible click on the air that doesn't sound good.

For *print interviews,* if you are going to have more than three people in three different locations on the call, use a conference call service to improve sound quality. Finally, do not use a phoner as an opportunity to multitask. Your full attention must be on the interview, not on sorting the piles of paper on your desk or answering e-mails. It also can be helpful to have a printed copy of your Key Message Points in front of you.

E-Mail

This type of interview is creeping into the mix more and more often. Usually, reporters will only use e-mail when they need to check a fact with a source who has already been interviewed in person or on the phone. Occasionally, reporters e-mail a single question to sources when they are doing a round-up type of story, in which they are canvassing many people about their opinions on a news event.

E-mail must be treated with the highest level of care because once you click on the "Send" button, it's out of your hands. One of my clients, a high-tech entrepreneur, was surprised when a reporter forwarded his e-mail to his reporting colleagues as well as to my client's competitors.

When a reporter e-mails a question, it is advisable to return the call by phone so that you maintain control.

Finally, remember that sometimes humorous e-mail doesn't translate well. You might think you are making a joke, but the reader could misinterpret your e-mailed comment.

In Person

When a reporter comes to your office, don't leave him waiting in the lobby. Go to the lobby and meet him in person.

Giving a quick tour of the office is a good way to break the ice. Ask the reporter is he or she wants something to drink, and then find a quiet place to hold the interview. It says some positive things about you if the interview takes place in your office, not in a sterile conference room. By having the interview in your office, you're sending the message that you are open and friendly. However, if you take this route, make sure you clean it up. Throw out your old lunches, and file any paper on your desk that you wouldn't want a reporter to read. When I was a reporter, I mastered the art of reading upside down. Whenever the source would divert his or her attention, I was reading away. Don't divert your attention. Try not to take phone calls (kids and spouses excepted).

Before the interview is even scheduled, find out how much time the reporter needs. Add 15 to 30 minutes to the reporter's estimate. Don't rush the reporter, but when time is up, if you need to move on to another appointment, offer to follow up within the next 24 hours with a phoner. If you don't need to stop the interview, then just let it flow for a while longer. If you set the interview for lunchtime (any time between 11:30 A.M. and 1 P.M.), order in some sandwiches.

Deskside Briefing

Deskside briefings are generally employed by company executives when they want to encourage magazine coverage of new products. Let's say a company is marketing a new kind of beauty product. Generally, the company public relations person calls every beauty editor of every magazine aimed at females and sets up deskside briefings so that you can introduce the product to the editor. For example, if the company is unveiling a new cream that makes wrinkles vanish, then the briefing might include the public relations person and the doctor or former model who invented the cream.

Editorial Board Meeting

If you're in a position where you are promoting a certain stance on an issue of the day, then it is often a good idea to ask for an Editorial Board meeting. You and your team—no more than three people total—would then go to the newspaper office for a meeting with the editorial page staff. Often, reporters who cover the issue for other sections of the paper are invited by the editorial page staff as well.

Everything you say in an editorial board meeting should be considered on the record and for attribution. Editorial Board meetings generally start with one of the senior newspaper staffers introducing everyone in the room. If the introductions don't happen, gracefully find a way to introduce yourself to those you don't know. Then, the senior newspaper staffer will start the meeting by asking a broad question. Leap into the answer and take an active role in guiding the resulting conversation.

Editorial page coverage is great if the newspaper's editorial board agrees with you. A negative opinion piece, however, can hurt your business. Don't wait for the Editorial Board to invite you to a meeting to discuss the pros and cons of the issue. Call the newspaper yourself and ask for the Opinion Department and then request a meeting with the editorial board. When you attend the meeting, be prepared for tough questions and make sure you bring any supporting evidence with you, such as academic studies or opinion surveys that shore up your position.

When then-California Governor Pete Wilson vetoed the funding for the State Bar of California, he said he was sending a message that the association of lawyers was playing politics instead of being a legal watchdog.

I worked with the Bar to help spread their message that the governor's veto was actually harming the citizens of California because the Bar didn't have the money to operate their investigative and punitive programs designed to protect citizens from unscrupulous lawyers. The way we mounted our campaign was to request Editorial Board meetings at every major newspaper. We attended every meeting armed with statistics and studies that proved our points. The resulting editorials didn't change Governor Wilson's mind, but it did help build support for the Bar so that a few months later, when Governor Wilson's term in office expired, the new governor approved the Bar budget.

Editorial Board meetings rarely last more than an hour. Bring some leave-behind collateral, such as a chart, fact sheet, or press kit.

Ambush

This is a favorite of television news magazines when the story is an exposé. The producer, camera operator, sound operator, and reporter race toward an executive who is usually leaving a courtroom, office building, or house. It can be overwhelming when all the executive wants to do is get out of the crush of people.

Don't put your hand in front of the camera and keep walking. When that footage appears on television, you will look guilty, guilty, guilty. It is as bad as saying "no comment." Instead, stop walking and make one of two choices:

Choice 1: Ask the reporter how much time he needs and if you can accommodate him, give him the interview.

Choice 2: Say that you really cannot comment on the situation, other than to say that it is a difficult time but you are confident that the mystery will be answered in the near future. Then say that now you are going to get in your car and go home because as much as you want to, you just can't talk about it. Often, in these situations, telling the reporter why you cannot grant an interview at this point is enough because it gives the reporter a soundbite to insert in the story.

Panel Discussion

Panel Discussions are a staple of conventions, conferences, and a great source of news for trade reporters. Generally, the moderator introduces the panel one by one, allowing each one to make some introductory remarks about the topic under discussion. The moderator then might ask a few follow-up questions before inviting the audience to ask questions. Don't say anything you wouldn't want to see quoted in the trade press.

In-Studio

The first time you walk into a television studio, try not to act surprised that it looks a little shabbier than it does on your screen. Watch your step—there are cables to trip over and heavy cameras to bump into everywhere you go. Whenever you see cameras and microphones, do not say or do anything you wouldn't want to see played back. There are plenty of instances when people have been heard uttering unpleasant things when they thought the microphone right in front of them wasn't hooked up. Moreover, microphones are designed to pick up the subtlest of sounds, so don't say anything you would regret.

When you sit down, make sure the back of your jacket doesn't ride up and create a roll on the back of your neck—take a tip that was immortalized in the James Brooks' film *Broadcast News* by sitting on the hem of your jacket. If your interviewer is sitting next to you, look at the camera, smile, and nod when you are introduced. From that point on, ignore the camera. Let the camera worry about finding you.

You don't need to do anything other than have eye contact with your interviewer and answer the questions. While the interview is going on, your interviewer might be shuffling papers or listening to the producer talking in his earpiece. Don't let the activity distract you.

Cameras can be intimidating, especially if you don't think of yourself as photogenic. To get past that negative way of thinking, decide that you are going to love the camera even if the camera doesn't love you. After all, when you send out a feeling of happiness, people watching pick up on it and as a result, they feel good about you.

If you are one of several people being interviewed simultaneously, try not to interrupt. Wait your turn—the host is there partially to make sure you get heard. In addition, always remember to keep your cool, even if one of the other people being interviewed is saying something incredibly ignorant. When a panel discussion show degenerates into a yelling match, nobody can hear anything anyone is saying and it becomes so annoying that many viewers switch channels.

There are also situations where you'll be interviewed in the studio, but the interviewer is located elsewhere. For example, perhaps the interview takes place in a studio in Los Angeles, and you are going to be interviewed by an anchor in New York. Sit in a chair, look straight ahead at the camera, and talk to the camera while hearing the questions in your earpiece. During the sound check, make sure to turn the volume up a little louder than you think you are going to need it. If the chair swivels or is on wheels, ask for a different chair, or, at least, ask how to lock it so that it does not move. If a television monitor is in your line of sight, ask the camera operator to turn the monitor so that you won't see it and it won't distract you.

During the interview, feel free to gesture with your hands from time to time. Otherwise, keep them clasped. After the interview, don't move out of your chair until the director or host gives you the all clear.

In-Studio Radio Interviews. Now let's turn to in-studio interviews with a radio host. In this situation, you'll wear bulky headphones.

There is so much equipment in radio studios that you might not even be able to see your host. If you can make eye contact, then do so.

During lengthy commercials, you can take off your headphones but pay attention, so that you don't miss the signal to put them back on. If your host has to push buttons and adjust dials during your interview, don't let the action distract you from your Key Message Points.

Radio interviewers often ask you to stay on for an extra segment to take questions from callers. Callers can be unpredictable and because they are often anonymous, many will ask tough questions or display emotion. Don't let that throw you; remember to bridge back to a Key Message Point. On both radio and television, move and talk a little more slowly than you normally would.

Responding to Different Reporters' Styles

Now that you know the different varieties of interviews and what to do in each situation, it is time to learn about different kinds of reporters. Give the same set of questions to two different reporters, watch them interview the same person and I will guarantee you two totally different interviews. That is because every reporter has a unique style. Some of the approaches you might encounter are discussed next.

The Dummy

This is the reporter who says he doesn't understand something and that is why he keeps going over the same ground. Don't believe it for a second. The reporter understands very well what you are saying; his goal is to get you to say something that is inconsistent so he can pounce on it later.

Business reporters employ this persona regularly, but don't fall for it. When one of my clients, a CEO of a public company, was prepping for an interview with a major business magazine, I warned him to beware if the reporter repeatedly said he didn't understand the company's information on their quarterly earnings and other numbers. Think about it: A reporter who covers business on a daily basis understands how to read quarterly earnings reports.

The What-If Reporter

This is the reporter who asks hypothetical questions. Watch out for hypothetical questions because there is too much speculation involved in answering them and therefore, too much danger that you might reveal personal feelings that you might want to keep private. It's far better to stick with the facts in the here and now. If a reporter asks a hypothetical question, what he's really looking for is a meaty answer from you. He's looking for you to slip up by asking how you would react if any number of unlikely events were to occur. You should answer, "I'm not too keen on answering hypothetical questions, because I can't read the future, but I get the feeling that what you really want to know is how I feel about this" and segue to a Key Message Point you want to talk about.

The Brand New Best Friend

Most reporters are people persons, so don't react suspiciously to every nice thing they say. However, some reporters appear overly friendly in order to get you to drop your guard. You might find yourself saying too much, and the reporter could surprise you by asking a highly personal question in a very blunt manner. When you recognize a reporter as The Brand New Best Friend, try to maintain a professional distance by staying in control of your Key Message Points and your answers.

The Machine Gunner

The Machine Gunner is a reporter who asks questions too rapidly to answer. The questions might be all about one subject, or they might

jump wildly from one subject to another. Gunners also might interrupt you mid-sentence to ask you something totally unrelated to
what you were just saying. Their real goal is to put you off balance
so they exert more control over the interview. Gunners are also
seeking to heighten the drama of a story and interview. Often, the
Machine Gunner style is employed when the interviewee is controversial. Don't fuel the fire by losing your cool in the face of rapid-
fire questions. Instead, politely say, "I'll be happy to answer that, but
first, I need to finish saying . . ." and maintain control over your behavior and over your Key Message Points.

Once during a live television interview, one of my clients, a
CEO of a public company that had recently laid off hundreds of
employees, was asked a series of questions by a Gunner, each question more contentious than the last. "Why didn't you try to find
other jobs for these employees? How can you give bonuses to yourself when you have put so many people out of work? Isn't this layoff
just an indication that your company is going downhill?"

Rather than becoming rattled, my client simply said, "You have
asked a lot of questions there. Let me go through them one at a time
because these are important issues." He didn't get defensive. He
didn't attack the reporter for demonstrating bias against his company. He knew that remaining calm and focused on his Key Message
Points would mean that the people watching the interview would
remember his answers and his facts, not the reporter's fireworks.

The Shrink and/or the Interpreter

This reporter is always rephrasing what you say. Sometimes he gets
it right and sometimes he doesn't, so listen to him carefully. If he
doesn't interpret correctly, then say, "Well, perhaps it is closer to
the way I feel if you describe it like this . . ."

The Interpreter isn't always seeking to get it right. From time
to time, an Interpreter will intentionally incorrectly restate your
answer just to heighten the drama of an interview. A reporter is always looking for a good quote and this is one way to get it.

The Silencer

Sometimes during an interview, particularly a television interview, you might finish saying what you want to say, and the interviewer remains silent. The Silencer thinks that if he refrains from speaking, then you will try to fill.

Silence makes many people uncomfortable. It might feel to you as if the silence is going on forever. It's probably just a couple of seconds. Instead of getting rattled and blurting out something you could regret, simply smile and say, "What else would you like to know?"

The Expert

A reporter who specializes in one particular field often tries to demonstrate his vast knowledge of your field. This type of reporter is always apparent at press conferences with airlines or NASA, where he asks a highly specialized question about the smallest possible detail, often to show you—and the other reporters present—that he knows his stuff. Keep in mind that in most cases, the Expert is really a reporter and generally not, truly, an expert about your field. Answer the specific question and then move into a more general area.

There may be some cases where the reporter has, in fact, been an expert in your field (plenty of journalists are on their second career) and the question might be too specific for the general audience. Answer the question quickly and bridge to a Key Message Point you want to highlight.

The Jester

The Jester is dangerous because you might be coerced into following his lead and joke around in return. However, you could end up saying something in jest that you would prefer not to have said to a reporter. During a taped interview, the Jester's remarks are usually edited out of the story and what is left is you making a joke that doesn't go over well. And during a live interview, it is too easy to get carried away. Get back on track by saying something like, "Well, it is easy to sit around and joke about it, but when I started this company, I really saw the opportunity to . . ." and move into one of your Key Message Points.

In summary, there are many aspects of the interview that are out of your control, such as the interviewer's style and what will happen to your interview during the editing process. Remember, the only thing you can control during an interview is your own behavior. Don't let yourself get rattled by the setting or the style of the questions. Remain calm and segue to your Key Message Points whenever possible.

KEY POINTS

➤ When you agree to an interview, remember to ask what kind of interview it is. Is it in person or on the phone? Is it an interview or a get-to-know-you briefing?

➤ During the interview, assess the reporter's interview style. Knowing why they are asking questions in a specific way will empower you because you will know that their questioning style is, usually, merely a tactic employed to heighten drama.

HOMEWORK

➤ Review the videotaped interviews you recorded and analyzed for your homework in Chapter 6, *Playing the Interview Game*. This time, when you watch the interviews, figure out which reporter personality fits the interviewer.

➤ Develop or track down some statistical information that you could provide to reporters that supports your company's position on an issue or business plan.

Things You Should Never Say to a Reporter

Lesson Plan

Now that you know what types of settings and interview styles you might face, we will discuss tactics for remaining articulate. We cover things to avoid saying to a reporter, and we also reveal ways to recover if you say something you immediately regret. As noted in past chapters, a reporter might be suspicious of you if you appear too polished; therefore, you can even make mistakes work in your favor.

Reporters often say that they are objective observers and not opinionated about the stories and the companies they cover. The truth is that reporters are people first. They get irritated and annoyed just like the rest of us. The best reporters try not to let their opinions creep into their work. Of course, as anyone who has been a target of a negative story will tell you, reporters don't always refrain from making subjective statements.

Things to Avoid Saying to a Reporter

Get your working relationship with a reporter off to a good start by recognizing what questions, gestures, and statements are most likely to irk a reporter or get you into trouble:

1. *This story you're doing will really help my sales/company/ negotiations.* A reporter doesn't write stories to help people. He writes stories because they are news. If the consequence of breaking the news is that something wonderful happens to someone in the story, so be it. Likewise, they don't take the blame if a consequence happens to be less pleasant.

2. *What's your angle?* "Angles" is one of those words that make reporters a bit grumpy. Reporters don't like to think that they have an angle going into a story, because that makes it sound like they have ulterior motives. The only motive they will ever admit to having is a desire to provide their audience with the truth.

3. *Here's my cell phone number.* This might seem like a good idea at the time. You think the gesture communicates the right amount of friendship and trust. Trust me, that cell phone number is going to ring and catch you off-guard at the worst possible moment, and the reporter on the other end is going to be asking you about an acquisition or a lawsuit or something else you can't talk about. If the reporter asks for your cell phone number, it is a much smarter move to tell him to e-mail you or call your office because you

check your messages every two hours and you will call him back ASAP if he has a last-minute question.

4. *Do you like what you've seen so far?* When put in such an awkward position, a real blood-and-guts reporter will say something noncommittal, like, "Well, it is certainly interesting." Alternatively, he will use the opportunity to ask another question. He won't give you his opinion, but he'll probably lose respect for you because you asked.

5. *Do you know what the headline will be?* Reporters don't write the headline and they get really tired of being asked about it. At many newspapers and magazines, there are employees whose primary responsibility is to write the headlines. Good headline writing approaches being an art. But in most cases, reporters have already gone home for the day when the headline writers get to work. Just like you, most reporters don't know what the headline is until it is published.

6. *I'll tell you off the record.* If you can't say something without first saying those six little words, then do yourself a favor: Don't say it at all.

7. *Let's go to Las Vegas (or Atlantic City or the bar down the street) and do the interview there.* Gambling and alcohol do not mix with presenting yourself and your company as responsible and investment-worthy. Seeing you lose a bundle at blackjack is just too juicey an anecdote to keep out of the story. Do you really want potential investors to conclude you have a cavalier attitude toward money?

8. *You weren't supposed to find that out!* As you know by now, all reporters are looking for the drama behind any story. By responding this way, you have just alerted the reporter that the information in question—that, by the way, they might not have been 100 percent sure about—is, in fact, 100 percent true. Also, because any story needs a slice of drama, you have let them know that this will fit the bill perfectly.

Avoid the situation by preparing in advance to answer embarrassing or controversial questions.

9. *Let me send you free tickets (or shoes or widgets or anything
else).* Serious reporters don't take freebies, and by offering
them gifts, you risk offending them. Even when it comes
to lunch, let the reporter pick up the check every once in
a while.

10. *I am not a crook.* (Other variations include: I never had sex
with that woman; I have not been a perfect husband.)
There is a pattern here. When you define yourself by saying what you are not, instead of what you are, it often
comes back to haunt you. When you phrase something
using a negative, it often provides fodder for the media for
years. For example, when he ran for his first Presidential
term, George H. W. Bush gave a televised speech and
vowed, "Read my lips: no new taxes." Once in office, however, he raised taxes and the media played and replayed
that pre-electrion promise because of the dichotomy between what he said and what he did.

11. *Did you get the fax?* I will talk about this more in Chapter
18 on how to pitch your company's story. For now, though,
it's enough to know that few questions set a reporter more
on edge than this one. For one thing, they are probably on
deadline. For another, it's a dead giveaway that you're a
public relations person pitching a story. All a reporter
wants to do when they hear that question is get off the
phone as quickly as possible. The reporter probably didn't
get the fax because fax deliveries at media companies are
notoriously faulty. If you snail-mailed the press kit, they
probably didn't get that either because in this post-Anthrax
Age, many media people ignore their mail. Therefore, send
the information via e-mail and rest assured that technology works. If the reporter is interested, you will be the first
to know.

12. *Can I see the story before it is published?* Reporters don't give sources an advance look at their stories. The best-case scenario is that they will check facts with you prior to publication. If you ask for an advance read of the story, the only thing you will succeed in doing is insulting the reporter and demonstrating your ignorance.

13. *To tell you the truth . . .* When you say this, you give the subliminal message that just maybe, you haven't been truthful during the rest of the interview. I also advise my clients to avoid saying, "to be perfectly honest" because it implies that they haven't been perfectly honest in everything they have already said.

14. *That bankruptcy/product failure/recall/big mistake was a learning experience.* If investors lost money or consumers lost their lives, it doesn't make the situation any more palatable that you learned something from it. Much better to admit that it was a huge mistake and that you are taking steps to make sure it never happens again. You can even say that you learned a great deal from the mistake, and that you suffered when it happened, but be careful not to dismiss it as a learning experience.

How to Recover from a Slip-Up

What if, despite all your preparation, something egregious slips out anyway? If a reporter noticeably bristles over something you say before or after the interview, don't make a big deal of his reaction. Instead, use it as an opportunity to say something humbling about yourself, like, "I guess that seems hard to understand to some people, but here is my thinking."

If you make a grammatical error or stutter on camera, don't let that slip derail you from making your key message points. You can easily recover by saying something like, "As you can see, I get so excited about our company that it makes me trip up on my words, but here is what I am trying to say."

Humility, especially in a newsworthy business executive, is a likeable characteristic.

Mistakes can actually help an interview because they make you seem more human. If you say something regrettable, don't dwell on it. Nobody likes a goody-goody who is always perfect.

Don't let making a mistake stop you from asking something you legitimately need to know. Some of the questions you should ask before every interview include:

- Do you know when your story is going to come out?
- Do you need any additional information?
- Is this a feature story or a trend story or a news story?
- What newspaper/magazine/television station/radio station did you say you worked for?

Now that you know what questions to ask in advance, how to avoid saying something that might irritate a reporter, and how to re-cover from inadvertent slip-ups, we turn in the next chapter to other ways to recover if the resulting coverage is not what you anticipated.

KEY POINTS

➤ Everything you say to a reporter, whether it is before, during, or after the interview, can affect your story.

➤ Give yourself every advantage to make a good impression.

➤ Avoid asking a reporter annoying questions or making statements that bely your ignorance.

➤ If you make a mistake, recognize the misstep as evidence of your humanity and move forward.

HOMEWORK

➤ When preparing for you next interview, make a list of five questions you can ask the reporter so that, in an effort to make conversation, you don't resort to the questions you should avoid asking.

CHAPTER

12

When Things Go Wrong

Lesson Plan

*There is a saying that journalism is history written on the run.
When history is written so quickly, there are bound to be errors.
There is, of course, a huge difference between minor mistakes
and journalism that is simply misguided and even libelous. In
this chapter, we discuss how to assess the press coverage that
you get and how to deal effectively with any conflicts you might
have with reporters.*

L et's say you have done everything right during your interview.
You treated the reporter with dignity, answered all her questions, remembered your Key Message Points, and felt good
about the interview.

Then the story comes out. And it is wrong, awful, and perhaps
even the death knell of your career.

Take a deep breath and get your blood pressure under control. Your plan should be to attack the situation in a logical manner and make sure to move carefully so that you don't make a bad situation any worse than it already is.

Get an Outside Opinion

The first thing you need to do is to call a good friend or trusted colleague—not somebody who will tell you what they think you want to hear. You need to call on a friend, relative, or coworker who will give you their honest assessment of the situation. This is the most crucial step.

Acknowledge that you might not be the best
judge of whether a story is accurate.

Here's an example from my personal experience about how subjective people's reactions to stories can be: One of my longtime clients started a new company, which was featured in a magazine article. Before the article appeared, my client was excited because he was in the process of trying to raise his next round of private investment. When the article came out, I read it, judged it to be accurate, and, on the whole, flattering. I then e-mailed the client and his senior staff to ask if they wanted me to send it to the company's list of prospective investors.

Within seconds, I received a rash of e-mails complaining about the story. Each e-mail was more emotional that the last. Each person who wrote stated unequivocally that the article was such a disaster that we needed to do our best to make sure no one ever read it.

I didn't understand—the story looked fine to me, and I am selective. I called the CEO and said, "I think I am missing something. I just don't understand why you all think this story is horrible for the company. Can you take a minute to point out to me what you think the fact errors are?"

"Sure," my client said. "I have it right here. And right in the first paragraph, it calls us 'fledgling.' That is negative."

"You *are* fledgling," I replied. "Your company has been in business for six months, you've raised less than $1 million in cash, and you have never produced a product. Fledgling isn't negative. It's a fact. It might not be the fact that you would choose to put out there about your company, but it is a fact."

As I have said previously, if you want an ad or a company brochure, then don't look for a reporter to produce it for you. If you want the credibility that comes with having your company spotlighted in a piece of journalism, then don't balk at the objective facts that the reporter might mention.

If the story is, on the whole, positive—meaning that the average reader will walk away from the story with an accurate perception of your company—then you have nothing to complain about.

It's very important to assess the story accurately. When I was a reporter, a source once called me to complain because I interviewed him for 30 minutes and the resulting story—about a wide-ranging trend—used only two quotes. He just didn't get the fact that even one quote in a national newspaper is the kind of exposure most business people crave. I never called the source for another quote. Another time, I had a client who complained because he believed his story belonged on the front page of a national newspaper, but the newspaper editors put it on page three. In both cases, the sources had unrealistic expectations.

If you can, put the article away and out of your mind for several hours. Sometimes, a bit of time allows people to more accurately judge a story about themselves.

If, however, the story was thoroughly damning and yours is a public company that has an obligation to shareholders to correct factual errors, you probably won't be able to buy yourself a little time.

What to Do When the Article Is Unfair

If the article is indeed unbalanced, then handle the situation carefully and calmly. If you step back from the situation and get an accurate assessment that the reporter either engaged in unethical or erroneous reporting, you might have a case to make. Handle your complaint with care, because journalists are naturally resistant to complaints from companies featured in stories. Reporters, editors, and producers know that company executives want a free ad instead of a piece of journalism. Therefore, if you don't handle the situation with care, journalists will discount your complaints.

Today, reporters and editors are more receptive than they ever have been to complaints from those they cover. In the past, news managers often thought that most complaints were so minor that they didn't deserve attention. That attitude was widely perceived by many story subjects as arrogance. Recent journalistic scandals—such as the 2003 revelation that plagiarism and lies permeated a *New York Times* rising star's stories—have served as a reminder to many editors that some complaints just might be justified.

Still, just as you have learned to control yourself and your message during interviews, you also must control the way you register a complaint.

I was working with one major company—listed in the Fortune 50—on a new product announcement when the company's vice president of public relations called me to get my opinion on another matter. As she explained, a top executive had been interviewed for a prestigious magazine. The interview was hitting the stands at that moment and it was riddled with factual errors and misquotes. The vice president had proof that the reporter had misquoted the executive, because the executive had taped the interview.

It sounded to me like there could be an opportunity to rectify the record. Then the vice president told me that she had already e-mailed copies of her letter of complaint to the reporter, the editor of the piece, and the publisher's office. Then she e-mailed it to me for my reaction and when I read it, my worst suspicions were confirmed. I knew that it would serve only to heighten the tension between the company and the publication, not defuse the situation or, more importantly, correct the record.

The primary mistake the vice president made was that her 11-page, single-spaced letter was overly emotional and overly detailed. Many of her objections were trivial, such as her complaint that the reporter was 10 minutes late for the interview. The trivial nature of many of the complaints ensured that the publication would not take her substantive complaints seriously. The reporter and editor would think that she had become too caught up emotionally to assess the article accurately. To make matters worse, the vice president had tipped her entire hand in the letter—she gave every bit of information she had. There was no new information to give the publication in any subsequent meeting.

E-mailing the complaint was also dangerous, because e-mails are so easy to forward. With a couple of keyboard strokes, the letter could be forwarded to hundreds of people, including other reporters, who could be enticed into covering the controversy.

How to Make the Situation Better When an Article Is in Error

Although it can be devastating when a reporter gets your story wrong, it is key that you handle the situation calmly and strategically, instead of instantly and emotionally. You don't want just to make the complaints—you want your complaints to be heard.

You want reparation, perhaps a commitment to publish your Letter to the Editor, or a correction. Here's a list of steps you should take:

1. *Make a list of your complaints.* To make your case, the first thing you need to do is make a list of every error in the story,

including names that are misspelled, facts that got twisted in the writing, and numbers that got transposed in the printing.

After you have the list, go back through it and make a new one. In this version, eliminate the minor complaints. For example, if the reporter says you drive a new car, but your car is a year old, that isn't a fact you want to complain about. Editors will perceive minor complaints as evidence that the client's bigger complaints are not justified. Too, if you complain about everything a reporter does, the editor will just conclude that the reporter merely hit a nerve because his reporting is so dead-on accurate.

2. *Calm down before you call the reporter.* Armed with your list, the best way to proceed is to wait a day or two, and then call the reporter. The waiting time will serve as a cooling-off period and allow you to be focused and unemotional. Before you make the call, know what you want as an outcome. As I have previously stated, some companies in some situations won't have the luxury of time. But in most situations, you can find five minutes to take a walk, cool down, and get your emotions under control.

If you merely want to inform the reporter so that they don't repeat their mistake in a future story, then having this as your goal will help you keep the tone of the conversation friendly and professional.

On the contrary, if the errors were so egregious that you want a printed or on-air correction, then you need to be up-front about asking for it in a calm manner. The last thing you want to do in this situation is to berate the reporter. Try saying something along the lines of, "Listen, it was great to meet you and I really enjoyed working with you on the story, and I thought you would want to know that there are a couple of misleading statements in there."

3. *Calmly review the errors.* Next, with your list in hand, go through the factual errors. Try to list the facts instead of engaging in a lengthy discussion about each one. If the reporter interrupts, listen and then calmly go back to your list.

Remember to strictly stick to the facts. For example, you might say, "You said our earnings are $2 million, when we in fact make $4.5 million."

Chances are, no matter how calm you keep your discussion, the reporter isn't going to admit to wrongdoing. Reporters are notoriously thin-skinned and they truly don't want the hassle of going to their editor and admitting they made a mistake.

4. *Enlist the editor if the reporter is unresponsive.* If, after your discussion, you believe that the reporter has not rectified the situation to your satisfaction, you are perfectly justified in approaching the editor. Again, remain calm and have your list in hand. When you call or e-mail the editor, assuming his office is close to you, ask for a convenient time for you to drop by for a meeting. If the editor asks for the purpose of the meeting, you can say that the story about your company contained some serious fact errors that you want to discuss. If the editor tries to ply the details out of you, say that you don't have time right now, but that you look forward to discussing it during your meeting. Assure the editor that you understand he's busy and that you promise to take just 15 minutes. The editor should agree to meet with you.

5. *Meet with the editor.* When you go to the meeting, don't be surprised when the editor asks the reporter to join the meeting. Stay calm and focused on your list. Do not give a copy of the list to the meeting participants until the meeting is nearing the end. You want the editor to be focused on the discussion, not reading the list.

The tone of the meeting should be professional, courteous, and nondefensive. The overall message should be, "Look, we just wanted to bring this to your attention because there are some pretty serious factual errors and we thought you would want to know about it."

Demanding that a new reporter be assigned to cover the company will most likely be met with refusal. Editors do not like to be told what to do. They believe in the adage that if you can't stand the heat, then stay out of the kitchen.

If the editor asks what the company wants, your answer should be along the lines of, "We want fair and accurate coverage. We are not looking for puff pieces—we just want to make sure that these kinds of factual errors don't hurt our company because we have an obligation to make sure that our clients/customers/students/

investors/vendors/employees/and so on know the truth about the company."

Usually, a calm, nondefensive approach like this will work. If, however, the reporter is truly unscrupulous and the editors are unwilling to listen and act accordingly, then you still have some options.

Other Options for Rectifying the Situation

The simplest option if all else fails is to write a letter to the editor. Make it brief and to the point as you enumerate the factual mistakes. These days, most publications don't have enough readers submitting letters to the editor, and hopefully, your letter will make the cut. Once your letter is published, make copies and put it in your press kit and make sure it is sent to your important clients.

If the letter-to-the-editor option does not right the wrong, then there are other, more serious options to explore. However, these options should be undertaken only by a public relations professional who has experience in such matters. There is an old saying, attributed to both Benjamin Franklin and Mark Twain, that you should never pick a fight with anyone who buys their ink by the barrel and newsprint by the ton.

One option is to locate someone who covers the journalism industry, such as a reporter for the *Columbia Journalism Review* or *Editor & Publisher,* and pitch the story to that publication. This might be challenging because reporters are quick to point out wrongdoing in every industry, but defensive of their own profession.

In fact, my former employer, Mike Sitrick, resorted to drastic measures when he had reason to believe that a television newsmagazine was doing a "hit piece" on one of his clients, who owned a controversial company. When the producer called to ask for an interview, Mike agreed as long as the producer wouldn't have a problem with the client videotaping the interview. The producer agreed, and the interview took place. As the airdate approached, Mike fielded follow-up questions from the producer, and the tone of the questions led Mike to conclude that none of positive aspects of the client's story would be included in the final story. Mike decided to take some drastic steps in order to preempt the interview. He created a web site and loaded the unedited video on it. In addition, he took out full-page newspaper ads in a national newspaper, inviting the public to go to the web site and view the whole interview so that they could get the whole truth.

The news magazine staff was stunned. No one had ever stood up to them in this manner before. But as we learned from several producers who were friendly with our firm, Mike's strategy caused the producer to reedit the story. The result was that the show aired a much more balanced story than the producer originally planned, and Mike was featured in a flattering story in several magazines, including *Forbes*.

A similar strategy, to be employed only when other, reasonable approaches have not produced results, and only when the reporter in question has a lengthy, negative track record, might be to set up an independent web site to gather all the various complaints lodged against the reporter, as well as any public notices of legal actions and news releases. When reporters have a track record of unscrupulous reporting, there is often a wealth of public information. With a web site that covers the reporter, it is easy to point other reporters to that site, thereby discrediting the reporter and anything the reporter has written about the client. This will also have the added benefit of putting reporters on notice that their professionalism is being monitored.

Prevent Things from Going Awry during an Interview

Perhaps the best strategy, though, is to prevent things from going wrong in the first place. The way to do that is to listen. (Remember, half of communication is listening.)

Usually, after an interview, reporters need to follow up with sources to verify a fact or ask an extra question or two. Those follow-up conversations can provide valuable clues as to how the story will turn out. In additional, major magazines, such as *Forbes*, and the *New Yorker*, send their stories through an extra fact-checking process. During this process, a representative of the fact-checking department—not the reporter—will call to verify every fact in the story, from the color of the walls in the CEO's office to the age of the company and how to spell every source's name.

Make a list of all the facts the checker is checking. Most fact-checkers start at the beginning of the story and work through it paragraph by paragraph, so the list you are keeping is a road map of the story. Correct all errors, no matter how minor they may seem to you because when an error comes out in print, it always seems bigger than life.

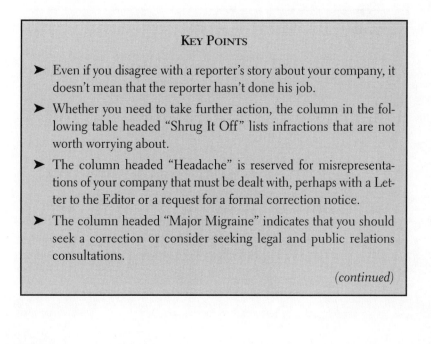

KEY POINTS

➤ Even if you disagree with a reporter's story about your company, it doesn't mean that the reporter hasn't done his job.

➤ Whether you need to take further action, the column in the following table headed "Shrug It Off" lists infractions that are not worth worrying about.

➤ The column headed "Headache" is reserved for misrepresentations of your company that must be dealt with, perhaps with a Letter to the Editor or a request for a formal correction notice.

➤ The column headed "Major Migraine" indicates that you should seek a correction or consider seeking legal and public relations consultations.

(continued)

KEY POINTS *(Continued)*		
Shrug It Off	**Headache**	**Major Migraine**
A description of your company that doesn't match what you would have written.	Factual errors, including a misspelled name or incorrect information.	Untrue and libelous statements.
An outside expert is quoted about your company. While you might believe their opinion to be ill informed, they have the right to state it.	An outside expert is quoted about your company and their statement is so damaging that you should respond.	A reporter who violates ethical journalistic practices, such as lying or breaking the law in pursuit of the story.

HOMEWORK

Read your local newspaper or an industry magazine and identify a story you disagree with. Write a fact-based Letter to the Editor that calmly lists the facts behind your opinion.

CHAPTER
13

Dress for
Media Success

Lesson Plan

Now that we have covered the words you will use to communicate your message, it is time to look at nonverbal communication. The way we dress and our body language supports or detracts from your Key Message Points. In this chapter, we cover how to dress and present yourself during interviews.

You've mastered the basics of communicating with the media, and now it's time to turn to another aspect of presentation: your appearance. The first ground rule is that although many offices have adopted casual dress codes, when we approach an interview, I encourage my clients to dress like an adult capable of leading their company and communicating their company's mission. This means that a suit is generally required for media interviews.

I watched a recent business-channel television interview with one high-tech CEO who went on the air wearing a red crewneck sweater. There was no lapel on which to clip the microphone, so it was clipped to the neckline, which made the neckline sag and resulted in an overall messy look. Plus, the CEO wasn't wearing a shirt under his sweater, so to the untrained eye of the casual viewer, it looked like the CEO was wearing a sweatshirt.

This was on a business television show, and one of the key audiences the CEO was communicating with was the Wall Street community who could invest in the company. Someone who looks like he threw on a sweatshirt doesn't immediately inspire confidence from bankers and investors who want to make sure that the CEO in charge of their investment is capable of making the company grow and prosper.

When you're in a suit, you present yourself as someone who doesn't take a casual attitude about your business. Wearing a suit shows that you have respect for the responsibility you hold, and it suggests that you are as serious about your work as you are about your clothing. Nobody looks like they're in charge when they're wearing a sweat suit—unless they accessorize with a whistle around their neck.

You might argue that Bill Gates doesn't wear a suit and tie. My response is that when you get to be Bill Gates, you won't have to, either. Until then, remember that clothing isn't just something you wear; it's a communications tool. If, for example, you want to communicate that your software company has come up with an indestructible virus detector and is therefore a good investment, then a missing button on your shirt or a wrinkled jacket contradicts that message by hinting that you can't be trusted to pay attention to details in your business, let alone pay dividends to investors, because you can't even manage to dress yourself appropriately.

> *The basic rule of thumb: Dress at least as*
> *well as the person interviewing you.*

Dress Appropriately for the Interview Setting

There are, of course, exceptions to wearing a suit. If you are giving *60 Minutes* a tour of your cattle ranch, if you are walking a local business reporter through your new warehouse, or if you are a government official touring hurricane wreckage, then dress appropriately. But remember: There is a huge difference between casual work clothes and stuff you wear to wash the car. If you're wearing khakis, make sure they are neatly ironed. Frayed jeans are fine if you are a rock musician or a fashion stylist. If you are not, then dress conservatively in tailored garments so that your words speak louder than your outfit.

Unless you work in a law firm or an investment bank, you probably don't wear a suit every single day. I recommend keeping a blazer, a fresh shirt, and a tie in your office.

If you are invited onto a television show because you are an actor, makeup artist, rock musician, or any other kind of pushing-the-limits creative type, you don't need to abide by the rules quite as strictly. You can wear jeans on camera as well as show off all your piercings and tattoos. One word of caution, however: Outfits that are over-the-top trendy live forever on videotape and can pigeonhole you and your act in a certain era, making it difficult for you to move on.

Stick with the Classics

Even if you are not part of the Hollywood crowd, these days, clothes are flashier than ever before. T-shirts are sprinkled with sequins and designers spray their products with logos. However, if you want to present yourself and your company as a force in your industry, then stick with the classics, like well-cut blazers, diagonally striped ties, cashmere sweaters, and colors like navy blue, camel, gray, and brown. Here are some more guidelines:

- Men need to take special care when choosing the spread of their jacket lapels and shirt collars and ties. Like hemlines on women's skirts, the width of lapels, the shape of shirt collars, and the width of ties constantly changes. Avoiding the extremes will help you and your company be perceived as classic, not overly trendy. Also, men sometimes choose a collar spread that isn't the most flattering for the shape of their face. Seek the opinion of an experienced tailor, and again, avoid extremes. One last caution on shirt collars: Men often keep buying the same shirt collar size that they have worn for years even though they may need to move up a size. If your collar is so tight that it bunches up when buttoned, it detracts from your message.

- Television cameras and the bright studio lights can exaggerate or minimize your appearance and clothing in unexpected ways. For example, if you have a blemish on your face, it probably won't be noticeable on television because the camera flattens out the image, but a lime green shirt might appear to be as bright as a neon light and a subtly patterned jacket might look overwhelmingly busy.

- On television, generally, everyone looks great in a navy blue suit.

- Avoid bright white shirts, because they don't photograph well. Almost everyone's face looks better surrounded by a more muted color because white next to your face can make your teeth and the whites of your eyes appear yellow.

- Red is another color that can be difficult for the camera to "read" and houndstooth and other small patterns can make the image "jump" or look squiggly.

- When you look great, you look comfortable as well, and looking comfortable speaks volumes before you even open your mouth.

You'll look comfortable in clothes that are clean, fit you well, and aren't calling too much attention to yourself. Clothes have to fit. Too-short sleeves and too-tight waistlines are uncomfortable and can distract you as well as your audience.

Choose Your Accessories to Complement Your Looks

Be careful about the accessories you choose. For example, in terms of your jewelry, anything that makes noise or dangles when you move will detract attention from your message. Here are some more tips:

- *Piercings and tattoos* are fine for models, rock stars, angry young actors, and anyone else who doesn't have to worry about distracting the interviewer (who will inevitably spend half the interview wondering exactly how painful it is to tattoo one's eyebrow).

- When it comes to *hats*, it makes sense to wear one if your interview is outside, where you might need to shield yourself from cold, rain, or the sun. Just make sure that the hat you choose doesn't cover too much of your face or look too costume-ish. Baseball caps are fine for athletes. Baseball caps worn backward are terribly clichéd. Stay away from most knit stocking caps because they make people look like they are about to hold up a liquor store.

- Men, please be aware that accessories like collar pins, suspenders, bow ties, and brightly colored pocket squares make a big statement. Be sure this statement is right for you.

Assemble Your Outfit in Advance of Your Interview

Make sure to give yourself plenty of time to select your interview outfit and to test it out. One way to make sure that you will look your most credible during an interview is to take some photos of yourself in several different outfits. Even better, videotape yourself answering some questions while wearing the camera-ready outfit you would wear for a real interview. Review the tape and photos with a critical eye. Make sure that the color of your jacket and the color of your shirt have enough contrast. Be certain that your tie isn't too busy. If you are a woman who wears pointy-toed high heels, make sure you are comfortable in them.

Don't Be Afraid to Be Stylish

Even with all of these rules, you can still appear pulled-together and stylish. In the 1980s and early-1990s, style for women on television generally stood still. They were generally advised to wear big, button-shaped clip-on earrings and bright jewel-colored suits with big collars and bold necklaces. Today, women on television—particularly, Katie Couric, Ann Curry, Greta Van Susteren, Ashleigh Banfield, and Judy Woodruff—have pushed those boundaries, and they've shown how they can appear professional and credible while wearing tasteful hoop earrings, sweater sets, eyeglasses, and softer, more natural hairstyles.

Generally, less is more. Stay away from jewelry that jingles and jangles and clothes that are too tight and too short. Use a light hand with makeup or you could end up looking like Tammy Faye Baker. Many women use a dark lip pencil and a lighter lipstick. It is a look that sometimes works in real life but looks horrible on television. Again, if you want to push the boundaries a bit, try on the outfit and tape yourself. A final note for women: Avoid dark hosiery. On camera, skin-colored hosiery always looks better.

Dressing for an Outdoor Interview

If your interview takes place outside, remember that people want to be able to look you in the eye to determine your credibility.

Therefore, shielding your eyes with a hat is preferable to hiding your eyes with sunglasses. If you must wear sunglasses, make sure the lenses are light enough to see your eyes through them. If you wear glasses for nearsightedness, then splurge on the nonglare coating so that people can see your eyes. Buy a new style of frames at least every two years to avoid looking dated.

Make Sure You're Well-Groomed

A special hurdle for many men is makeup. Because of the bright lights, everyone on television looks better with a little face powder and a touch of lip cream. Many male executives shake their heads over this at first, but once they sit in the makeup chair, they like being groomed because it makes them feel more confident. Whenever a client complains about wearing makeup, I assure him that I have a packet of oil-free makeup remover wipes (available at any drugstore) in my briefcase and he can wipe the makeup off immediately following his television appearance.

Finally, make an accurate appraisal of yourself in terms of your grooming. Ask your barber to help you—he will tell you if your eyebrows are overly bushy or if your mustache needs a trim. If your nails are ragged, get a manicure (for men: buffed, no polish; for women: short, light-color lacquer). In addition, it isn't hard to find a wardrobe stylist to help you—nearly every department store has one. Not everyone is blessed with good taste and consulting with a reasonably priced stylist is economical in the long run, because it helps you avoid spending money on unflattering attire.

As for your daily uniform, you need to remember that your employees and customers—the people you come in contact with every day—are also audiences with whom you want to communicate positively. Dress respectably, avoiding things that are too high, too short, too loud, too old, or too bright. The quality and condition of your shoes is always noticed. A person wearing a blazer always looks like he or she is in charge.

Body Language

Clothing isn't the only thing that matters during interviews. The way you gesture and your posture make a big impact as well. Here are some common body language guidelines:

- *Slouching* during an interview reduces your energy level. Sitting up straight improves the projection of your voice and communicates confidence and forthrightness.

- *Gesturing too much* can make you appear nervous and, therefore, less credible. It also distracts from your message. On the other hand, never employing a hand gesture appears unnatural. Also, when you're not gesturing, keep your hands folded and in view.

- *Repeatedly crossing and uncrossing your legs* is a common reaction to the stress of an interview, but it is distracting and probably will serve only to increase your nervousness.

- *Sitting too far back in your chair* can make you appear to be defensive. Sitting back in your chair while holding your fingers in a "steeple" position communicates arrogance.

- *Biting your lip or clenching your jaw* while listening to a question indicates you are afraid of the question and might be trying to hide something.

Slang Expressions

All of us have our own signature speech patterns and sometimes, those speech patterns need a bit of modification. When I appeared on television during the O. J. Simpson trial, I noticed that I said "ummm" too much. The effect was that it made me appear unprepared or unsure of what I was saying. Often, when tics like that are pointed out to us, our awareness generates a reduction in that behavior. Finally, using trendy expressions—like "Whassup" and "Awesome" during an interview can appear less mature than you would like to project.

KEY POINTS

Dos

Classic colors (navy blue, beige, gray)
Shined shoes
Relaxed facial expression
Hats (if the weather and occasion warrant)
Nonglare eyeglasses
Ties on men, especially if being interviewed about their business
Controlled, yet relaxed, hand gestures; nodding your head when
  introduced on camera
A good watch and/or a small amount of classic jewelry (silver or gold
  hoops)
Tasteful scarf
Cuff links (as long as they are not flashy)
Groomed nails that look natural
Suit
Tasteful makeup

Don'ts

Houndstooth and other small prints
Wrinkled clothes
Facial piercings
Dark sunglasses
Broken, crooked, or out-of-fashion eyeglass frames
Too much red (unless you are dressed in a costume)
Shiny fabrics
Garish jewelry
Key Message Points: Only in your head; never written and in your
  hand during an interview
More than one assistant
Bright nail polish
Collar pins
Women's colored hosiery or opaque tights; ill-fitting socks on men
  (no gaps between pants and socks, please)

(continued)

KEY POINTS *(Continued)*

Maybes

White (in small doses)

Jeans (creative types only)

Visible tattoos (performers and WWE stars only)

Clothing with noticeable designer labels or slogans (make sure it is a message with which you want to be forever linked)

Bed head (performers and models only)

Pocket squares and tie clips

Hair spray (keep it on the light side)

Earrings that dangle (again, allowed for musicians and actors)

Your attorney (advised in sensitive situations)

Ties on women

Nail polish in trendy colors like black, or patterns, like polka dots

Leather jackets (If you represent a business, leather is only allowed if it is of a classic design and not black.)

Lower-cut shirts on women (unless you want everyone to be looking at your cleavage instead of listening to you)

HOMEWORK

➤ Stock your office with a spare, interview-ready outfit just in case a last-minute media opportunity arises on the day you're casually dressed. (Sometimes, it seems like the perfect media opportunity arises on the day you are moving your office!) Men's spare outfits should include a conservative tie, clean shirt, and blazer. Women's spare outfits should include a clean shirt, blazer, and an extra pair of hosiery. Everyone should make sure his or her desk is stocked with a small sewing kit (including spare buttons) and a lint brush.

➤ To cut down on unnecessary body movement, practice sitting still for five minutes at a time.

PART FOUR

IMPLEMENTING MEDIA TRAINING ON THE FLY

When the Media Just Shows Up

Lesson Plan

In this chapter, we discuss how to react if a reporter shows up unexpectedly at an event or at your office. We cover tactics for handling the media when you have not had an opportunity to plan—or a second to think.

When the media just shows up, it can be a good thing or a bad thing. For the most part, the outcome depends on you, not the journalists standing there, waiting at your front door.

You are responsible for the outcome when the media just shows up—you can remain calm and respond intelligently, or you can shirk away or become infuriated. Remember, a reporter's questions don't matter nearly as much as your answers, and you can only control yourself and your behavior.

Naturally, there are some circumstances that are inherently better than others, and if a reporter from *60 Minutes* surprises you in your office parking lot, spouting rapid-fire questions that sound like accusations, this is not nearly as pleasant as if a reporter arrives unannounced to cover your company's sponsorship of a charitable fund-raiser. However, either situation is not a slam-dunk. Just because Ed Bradley is catching you by surprise doesn't mean you can't take the opportunity to communicate the message you want to put out to the world, and just because a reporter is covering your fund-raiser for a good cause doesn't mean that you can't say something you later regret.

Generally, when the media catches a source by surprise, the situation falls into one of four categories, which are listed in order of the potential difficulty they present:

1. Showing up for a good cause
2. Talk radio is calling
3. Deadline dialing for quotable reactions
4. Ambushing the hard-to-get source

Showing Up for a Good Cause

Let's say you are hosting a charity event and, although you sent the media invitations and followed up with a Media Alert and called the Assignment Desk, you never heard a word from them. And now they are here.

This is a common scenario, particularly if your charity event is exciting or will be visually stimulating on camera. Events that garner media attention might include a 1950s-style dance marathon, a head-shaving party to raise money for children's cancer research, or a celebrity golf tournament. Often, local television news operations cover such events by sending a camera crew without a reporter, who is probably tied up covering a local government meeting or a crime wave. Sometimes, a journalist and a crew show up because another story fell through, or a small newspaper editor might send an intern, who didn't have time to call first.

Here's how to handle this situation: First, take a deep breath. Visualize your Key Message Points. Remember that any media opportunity that reflects well on you will also reflect well on your company. There might even be an opening for you to mention your business and why your company has gotten involved in the charity.

Remember, even if this media opportunity does not result in press that extols your company, it still gives you the opportunity to make media contacts that could help you secure another story down the road. Moreover, the more positive press you are connected with, the better your own reputation and media profile.

Go over and shake the journalist's hand and welcome him. Ask if he would like to interview you or the charity's executive director about the event. Enlist a colleague's help and while you are talking with the reporter about what he needs to do his job, your colleague can round up the needed sources. Throughout the story-gathering process, someone from your event should be available to the reporter to assist him in getting every element he needs for the story.

Finally, make sure you set any limits that you see are necessary. For example, if the reporter asks if he can interview the local celebrity/guest of honor backstage, then you need to find out—outside of the reporter's presence—if that's acceptable with the guest of honor. If the celebrity declines to do a one-on-one interview, then perhaps he would let the crew tape his remarks or agree to hold a press conference following the event.

Talk Radio Is Calling

Often, when a story is published in a newspaper or magazine, it catches the attention of a talk radio host or producer. As a result, you might receive a call from a talk radio producer who wants to put you on the air right now.

Don't get rattled; get ready. Here's how.

First, when you know a story is scheduled to be published about your company, make sure that whoever answers the phones at your office knows what do and how to reach you when producers or other reporters want to follow up on the story. Inform the person who answers the phone that radio producers are typically aggressive because their jobs depend on getting an immediate response. If a producer calls and asks to speak with an executive director and then is transferred to voice mail, he will instantly call back, demanding to speak to a live person. If a producer's phone behavior is less than polite, have the person answering your phone buy some time by telling the producer they will call back in a few minutes. Use these few minutes to decide whether this is an opportunity you want to accept.

You need to give serious thought as to whether you should proceed with the show. These days, talk radio is all about the hosts, not about the guests, and successful shows showcase their hosts. These shows act as a forum for allowing the host to espouse his set of principles. For example, among other philosophies, John Kobylt and Ken Champeau, hosts of *The John and Ken Show*, the number-one rated afternoon drive-time radio show in Los Angeles (the nation's biggest radio market), believe that working Americans are tired of being victimized by political gamesmanship and partisan politics. They employ a common-sense view of the world and advocate simple solutions for problems, like banning carpool lanes to alleviate freeway congestion and the immediate dismissal of Catholic bishops who oppose cooperation with police investigating molestation cases.

If your views are aligned with John and Ken's views, then great. Your interview will be likely be short and complimentary, and it might represent an excellent opportunity for you to validate your story. If, however, your views run counter to their well-known and often-espoused tenets, then get ready for a bit of a rough ride. For example, politicians who advocate studying the problem before suggesting a solution are likely to fuel John and Ken's scorn. Argue with them and your defensiveness will only fuel their attacks on your position. In contrast, exhibit a sense of humor and say something along the lines of, "Well, I understand that we see things a bit differently on this, and we believe that reasonable people can disagree on this. But I want to assure you and your listeners that we have given this matter a lot of thought and we truly believe that the facts show that we're doing the right thing for our customers, our employees, and our stockholders."

State your beliefs passionately, but keep your emotion—
especially anger and defensiveness—in check.

In addition, remember that you don't have to accept every media opportunity that comes your way. Talk radio moves very swiftly. The producer who calls because he read your company's story is also calling several other potential interviewees. When he calls you, take a moment to gauge whether this opportunity is right for your company. If it is not, then have your representative call back in a few minutes and say that you simply can't make the interview. However, if you turn down the interview, be aware that the host might talk about your story anyway, and you won't have a chance to comment or communicate your own story. It's a balancing act, and only you know what's right for you and your company.

Deadline Dialing for Quotable Reactions

Sometimes, you just can't plan for the best media opportunities. When I was a reporter at *USA Today*, any significant national event could trigger what is called a "round-up," or a story about the way people across the country are reacting to a particular news event.

As you might expect, reporters have an off-color name for this kind of story. They call it a "gang-bang" because a gang of reporters is put on the story and given a tight deadline. They then furiously call anyone and everyone they can think of who might have something to say about the subject.

We saw a lot of this kind of reporting during the war against terrorism. For example, when the federal government advised U.S. citizens to stock up on emergency supplies like duct tape and plastic sheeting, reporters across the country called a variety of sources for their reactions to the warning. The ensuing stories quoted hardware store owners who said they couldn't keep up with the demand, parents who said they were instructing their kids on what do in an emergency, psychologists who commented on the anxious state of the population—in other words, anyone who could speak to the issue.

When a news event occurs that happens to affect your business, you could get a call. Perhaps your company's last three press releases didn't get a lot of coverage, but a reporter might remember that your company is in an industry that is uniquely affected by the news, whatever it might be. In these instances, it is important to remember that you have only five minutes to decide whether the media opportunity is right for your company. When that reporter's call comes in, tell the reporter that you are tied up for a few minutes, but you will call back. Take those moments to review your Key Message Points and ascertain whether the media opportunity is one that you want to accept. Ask yourself if it make sense for your company to participate. Regardless of what you decide, call the reporter back. Do the interview or tell the reporter that the subject matter does not pertain to your company. If you are going to turn down the opportunity, have a suggestion of someone else the reporter should call.

When I was a vice president of a high-tech company that had begun the process of becoming publicly traded, I got a call from a prominent business reporter with whom I had worked on several stories. The reporter told me that she was following up on the recent news that several public high-tech companies had experienced such steep drops in the price of their stock that they were giving employees more stock options or lowering the employee stock purchase price as a way to keep morale up. She wanted to know what my company was doing to combat the stock drop.

I thought about it for a minute and decided it just wasn't a news situation that pertained to my company. For one thing, we weren't public so our stock options were still theoretical. In addition, our company had been valued just two weeks ago and the valuation remained consistent with our option program. We just didn't fit the story, but I did tell the reporter that I had seen a press release from a different company that might fit the bill.

If you do participate in the interview, remember that it does not guarantee that your quote will make it into the final story. In fact, it's likely that the reporter interviewing you is not the reporter in charge of putting all the quotes together and writing the story. However, this fact alone shouldn't stop you from participating, and even if your quote doesn't make it into the story, reporters fondly remember sources that help them out on deadline. That fondness won't guarantee you coverage, but it could make the difference between whether a reporter listens to your next story pitch.

Ambushing the Hard-to-Get Source

As you have seen throughout this book, dealing with the media is often more of an art than a science. Journalists are often unpredictable.

However, there is one immutable fact that you can count on: Ambushes are never a good thing.

If nothing else, ambushes are dramatic, and, as you learned in Chapter 4, drama is an essential—if not the most important—element of any story.

Think about how many *60 Minutes* stories about corporate scams feature a correspondent running through a parking lot, trying to get the company CEO to talk to him. Invariably, the camera shots always include the executive trying to hide his face from the camera or demanding that the crew get off company property and turn the cameras off immediately. The result is that the ambushee always appears guilty. Even worse, Ed Bradley, Steve Kroft, or Leslie Stahl then talk into the camera explaining that they tried by phone, fax, e-mail, and Pony Express to set up an interview, but the executive didn't respond, the appearance of guilt often becomes the fact indelibly imprinted in the viewers' minds.

Now you know what not to do, but knowing *what to do* is a bit trickier.

When you or your company is the object of an ambush interview, it is a pretty clear signal that the story is most likely devoid of any positive reporting about your company. Your only choice at this point is to say something or not. Not talking probably won't be perceived as well as if you say something.

Your statement doesn't have to contain a lot of substance. It can be a simple statement that "We are in the business of providing the highest quality service to our customers and we would like to assure the public that their faith in us is well-placed." Chances are that if that is the only statement you make, it will be included in the finished piece and at least you will have communicated your side to your employees, customers, and supporters.

Whatever you do, do not put your hand over your face or over the camera. If you can, stop walking for a moment and say something like, "I can't talk about this now but I hope to be able to soon. Right now, I need to go to work so that is what I am going to do." Then keep your mouth shut and walk purposefully into your office.

Radio and print reporters can also take part in ambushes, particularly in situations when the person being ambushed is connected to a controversial figure in the news.

For example, let's say a major business executive has just been accused of insider trading. Most likely, reporters will convene en masse at the executive's office, hoping to get an interview or a comment or a photo of the shamed executive running from his car to the office.

Refusing to talk isn't going to make the
reporters go away. Instead, it's merely going to fuel
the coverage in which your side is not represented.

In such situations, it is always better to for a spokesperson to go outside and make a statement to the press, such as, "This is a difficult day for us. We know that once the investigation is concluded, our company will be fully and completely exonerated. But right now, we are not able to answer your questions. We will issue a press release if there is a significant development that we can comment on. In the meantime, we are going back to running our business and serving our customers."

By delivering a statement like this, you are able to help define a story that your company is starring in, like it or not. If the media is going to cover you and your company, with or without your cooperation, it's better to communicate your side instead of hoping that someone else will do it for you.

Should you ever need to write such a statement, here are the goals to strive for:

- Let reporters know that you are not going to be saying anything more for a while, so they can leave the stakeout without fear that they will miss anything significant.
- Let customers know that this situation is not disrupting your company and that you are doing business as usual.
- Let the public know that your company is not just a monolith — it is made up of humans. You are saying, of course, this is a difficult day. But we are doing our best to run our business because we know we are innocent of these spurious charges.
- Let prosecutors know that you are reasonable but not intimidated.

KEY POINTS

➤ The way you handle an unexpected media demand determines, to a large extent, the tone of the story.

➤ If you look like you are avoiding the press and the public, you will look guilty.

➤ If you turn down an unexpected media opportunity, be prepared to take the fall-out.

➤ You should also review each opportunity carefully in order to determine if it's right for you and your company.

HOMEWORK

With a trusted colleague, or with your public relations person, discuss how you would handle the unforeseen media opportunities mentioned in this chapter: Showing Up for a Good Cause, Talk Radio Is Calling, Deadline Dialing for Quotable Reactions, and Ambushing the Hard-to-Get Source.

Meet with your frontline person—your receptionist, in-house public relations person, or office manager—and establish guidelines about how to handle unannounced press visits or phone calls.

Crisis Control

Lesson Plan

*Every business has its ups and downs. In this chapter, we ex-
plain how to prevent losing face during a crisis by forming a
Crisis Committee and developing company policies. I'll also
discuss how to manage handling the crisis while remaining calm
in front of the press.*

C rises are a natural part of the life cycle of any company. Un-
predictability is simply a part of doing business. Nobody can
foresee every situation that might arise; and no one can prevent external disasters that could affect your company.

The unpredictable nature of crises impacts the way a company's
public relations experts handle the issues. Because every sensitive
situation is different and every company has unique qualities, products, and structures, there simply isn't a quick fix that fits every situation. Still, there are constant themes that run through the
effective handling of corporate public relations emergencies.

The most important thing to know about controlling a crisis is how to prevent one. Unfortunately, much—if not most—of the time, that is something you learn only in hindsight. The same people who never contribute during the decision-making process are usually the first ones to tell you where you went wrong and how they saw trouble coming from miles away.

Their observations might be given with the utmost sincerity, but it doesn't do you any good when you have a big problem to solve and your company is in jeopardy. It only makes focusing on the problems that much more difficult. Too many could haves, would haves, and should haves will distract you from finding a solution to the immediate problem. Before you find your company embroiled in a crisis, I'll tell you what I have learned by helping dozens of companies in the middle of public relations crises.

Crisis Preparedness Strategies and Tactics

One public company went into crisis when its CEO discovered that he had terminal cancer and was given only a few weeks to live. In addition to the looming tragedy of losing their leader, there were no plans for a successor. When the company informed the Wall Street community about this significant development—as federal securities law requires—the company risked losing investor confidence and commitment. Those very real worries could have been avoided if the organization had established a Crisis Committee that regularly issued accurate and honest assessments of its vulnerabilities.

> *Give yourself a head start on handling a crisis*
> *by appointing a Crisis Committee. Empower*
> *that committee and take it seriously.*

Taking it seriously means you don't reschedule the meetings just because a deadline is approaching on a different project. The committee should meet at least once a month to work through exactly how you would react if your company were to be disrupted by an earthquake, a fire, a disgruntled employee, revelations of shareholder or vendor wrongdoing, a drastic slide in your stock price, or anything else you can think of. The discussions should be frank and confidential. Membership of the committee should include rank-and-file employees as well as senior managers. Front-line employees often see crises looming before senior staff do because they are the ones dealing with customers day-to-day. Also, during a crisis, it is important for other front-line employees to feel that they are represented at the highest levels. Just make sure that everyone you select for the Crisis Committee is trustworthy and will not blab about confidential matters.

You company's Crisis Committee should practice and videotape question and answer sessions for various potential scenarios. The beginning of the videotaped session would begin with a member of the Crisis Committee reading a potential scenario. A sample scenario, for a high-speed Internet services company—let's call it High Speed Connect—based in Los Angeles could go like this: "This morning at 10:45, Southern California experienced a 7.1 earthquake that caused widespread damage to the region. High Speed Connect's network was affected by this severe earthquake. Approximately 90 percent of our customers lost their Internet service. Twelve High Speed Connect employees were injured when the earthquake struck and several heavy computer servers fell. One employee is in critical condition at Mercy Hospital. The other 11 have been treated and released. At this time, service has been restored to 20 percent of the customers affected by the earthquake. We do not have an estimate of when service will be restored to our entire customer base."

One member of the Crisis Committee writes the scenario and keeps it secret until it is read out loud to the entire group. After reading the scenario, the company spokesperson—the public relations consultant or the chief executive—sits in the hot seat and the video camera is turned on.

The other Crisis Committee members then pretend that they are reporters, firing questions about the crisis. The question session should last 10 to 20 minutes and cover all aspects of the scenario as well as general questions about the company. When it is over, the entire group should watch the videotape and offer suggestions about how the person in the hot seat could better answer the questions and improve his credibility while projecting confident and sympathetic body language.

The Crisis Committee chairperson should put together a notebook that includes essential facts about the company, including the number of employees, the year the company was founded and other basic questions journalists would be likely to ask. Include a phone list so that the Crisis Committee can reach one another around the clock. Also include sample press releases for various crisis scenarios so that you will have a template to help guide you during an emergency.

In the event of a civil emergency, such as an act of terrorism or a natural disaster such as a flood, fire, or earthquake, decide how and where the Crisis Committee can operate. When the Crisis Committee chairperson is out of town or otherwise unavailable, decide who is going to step into the role.

The members of the Crisis Committee should receive two copies of the crisis notebook. They should keep one copy at the office and the other in their car or at home so that if a crisis occurs outside of business hours, the information is available.

If crisis planning is too much for your company to take on internally, hire a public relations company to write your plan and prep you.

The most important aspect of crisis planning is that your company's crisis plan should be a living document. Don't just relegate it to the bottom of the pile in your In Box. Review it at least once every six months and revise it as needed.

There are, of course, many different crises your company might face, from serious meltdown to employees who attract negative press. Some advice for avoiding crises follows. We also discuss ways to implement strategies for handling crises, before they transpire.

Crises to Avoid and Ways to Preempt Them

Avoid Becoming Too Confident

One crisis to avoid is having an employee become conspicuously overconfident. How many times have you watched some business person become a superstar, quoted in all the magazines and admired on all the talk shows, only to fall? And when they fall, they fall hard.

When you start believing that your job is to be a media darling instead of running your company, it's a hop, skip, and a jump to when the media starts writing and reporting unflattering things, thereby triggering a crisis.

Some public relations experts say this happens because the media builds someone up only to tear them down. I think it's more complicated than that. Every reporter aims to write the story that everyone else overlooked. Reporters want their stories to be new, fresh, and different. If everyone is writing raves, then it is just a matter of time before a reporter comes along who sees things a bit differently and, as a result, writes a different story.

Develop Appropriate Policies

Often the best defense for a company that is under fire is to offer proof that the situation was not of the company's making and that the company is the victim of this scandal, not the villain. A company can avoid being dragged into many scandals by developing the proper policies to protect its reputation. For example, one company I worked with was shocked to discover that an employee had been arrested by FBI agents allegedly for running an Internet pornography business on his office computer. The company had a clear, written policy against using company computers or telecom systems to transmit sexual content. The company also had a clear record of conducting regular investigations and semi-annual audits of employee computer usage. (The alleged activity had taken place between those regular audits.) These policies helped assure that the company could point to its actions as proof of the company's record for noninvolvement.

Discuss potential policies with your company's Crisis Committee as well as your corporate counsel, and make sure you cover a range of possible scenarios.

Be Mindful of the Brother-in-Law Rule

The Brother-in-Law Rule is that in a group of, let's say, 30 people, one of them knows or is related to a reporter. Therefore, once a company's secret is known by more than 30 people, a reporter somewhere is going to somehow find out.

A good reporter breaks stories because people leak the details.

When your company is involved in a situation that is likely to become public knowledge, often you can gain the upper hand by announcing the news yourself. Make sure the announcement includes the steps your company is taking to investigate and fix the problem.

Avoid Conflicts of Interest

Even the slightest *appearance* of a conflict of interest can cause a crisis.

Public relations people say that often perception becomes reality; that is, if it looks like your company has done something illegal, many people will believe the worst. For example, a politician who accepts a campaign donation from a developer who, the next day, is awarded a multibillion dollar state contract, is going to be written about. The politician will have a public relations crisis to handle and so will the developer. Most likely, the developer also will find it difficult to obtain future contracts from the government.

Use Your Own Product

If a movie star is the spokesperson for Coca-Cola and a tabloid gets a picture of the star sipping a Pepsi, it gets published. The message of such coverage is that the product is endorsed in name only. In addition, if you are your own consumer, then you'll know the problems before anyone else.

That is why so many cutting edge products get onto the marketplace without being fully understood—let alone used—by the company's senior staff. If you are the CFO for a company that sells camera-equipped cell phones, you need to know how they work, in addition to knowing the amount of the company's cash on hand.

Increase Oversight

If you are a public company, make sure that the people in charge of meeting or exceeding analyst expectations are not the same people in charge of the audit.

Safeguard your company with separate
sales and auditing procedures.

Make sure your company's accounting practices are impeccable and don't take shortcuts. Accuracy should be your primary objective. In the accounting scandals of 2002–2003, many companies, like Enron and Tyco, hid their expenses and inflated the companies' bottom lines. By mid-2003, some companies, eager to avoid such scandals, began under-estimating their profits, which also brought sanctions and investigations because investors were denied the accurate information they need in order to make an intelligent decision about putting their money into the company's stock.

Crisis Response Tactics and Strategies

Preparedness is not a talisman of protection. Even the most well-run and prepared companies face unforeseen and unpreventable acts and misdeeds. When you find your company in the unwanted spotlight, follow the tenets of strategic crisis handling that we discuss next.

Try to See the Opportunity

It might be hard to see it at first, but any crisis is an opportunity for better public relations in the future. For example, when I was consulting for the State Bar of California during a funding crisis, we were able to use media opportunities to talk about the Bar's consumer protection initiatives and the Bar's programs to provide drug and alcohol rehabilitation services to lawyers whose addictions had caused them to be derelict in their client responsibilities.

As another example, when the recession first hit the high-tech industry, causing massive layoffs, many companies issued press releases that just stated the grim facts and focused on the number of employees now out of work. When the high-tech company I was part of had to announce layoffs, we saw the opportunity to talk about our commitment to responding quickly to the changing market conditions. We acknowledged that we would miss our former colleagues and regretted that the company was forced to move forward without them. We emphasized the fact that we had a responsibility to our investors and customers to operate our company in a fiscally responsible manner. That responsibility meant that we must respond to the unfortunate economic climate. The resulting coverage about our layoff centered on the company's agility to adjust our business to respond to the changing economic picture.

Acknowledge the Elephant in the Room

Companies often make a crisis worse by refusing to acknowledge to a reporter that the crisis, in fact, exists. I believe that was one contributing factor to Martha Stewart's insider trading accusations. At the beginning of the investigation, the diva of homemaking was demonstrating a salad recipe on a morning television show when she was asked about the recently revealed scandal. Ms. Stewart refused to answer any questions or acknowledge that her company was feeling any fallout from the federal investigation into her finances. She said that she just wanted to continue making her salad—and that soundbite, which appears to demonstrate arrogance, has been replayed thousands of times. She even resigned from her regular appearances on a television morning show, rather than address any questions. Her refusal to acknowledge that her company was in a crisis only made reporters more determined to write stories that detailed every new development. It would have made a difference if she had been more forthright instead of appearing to go into hiding because it made it look like she thought she was above answering the questions.

One clear example of an executive who acknowledged the elephant in the room is Howard Luster, the CEO of Cantor Fitzgerald, the Wall Street firm that lost hundreds of employees in the World Trade Center attacks on 9/11.

Immediately following the attacks, Luster appeared on television, acknowledging the devastation of his company. He cried as he discussed the loss of life and the challenges his company faced in its rebuilding efforts. He pledged to do his best to rebuild his company and maintain his commitment to the families of his lost employees. Today, Cantor Fitzgerald's rebuilding efforts have restored the company's prominence and profitability.

Involve Your Company Lawyer

Many crises involve legal issues and complications. What can first appear to be a straightforward situation can be complicated by legal concerns that your lawyer can foresee. Openly discuss your crisis plan with your legal team and be prepared to make adjustments based on the team's recommendations.

Separate Marketing and Public Relations

When your company is in the middle of a public relations crisis, you need credibility more than ever. Reporters tend to find marketing executives to be less credible than an attorney, the chief executive, or the company spokesperson.

The person in charge of answering reporters' questions should be in charge of issuing company news, not meeting sales projections. Also, if your company's public relations person is not an integral part of your senior team, then it is time to make a change.

Don't Wait for Things to Get Better

If you need it, spend the money to hire strategic counsel at the earliest possible moment. Once a crisis spins out of control, it could be impossible to regain the upper hand.

Other Tactics for Dealing with a Crisis

Although each crisis has its own unique elements, many share common characteristics and many crisis consultants specialize in particular business crises. For example, if your company is filing bankruptcy, there are some public relations consultants who have handled the communications for dozens of similar filings. These consultants know the common pitfalls to avoid because of their experience.

Finally, once the crisis is over, move on. At the beginning of the crisis, it might be appropriate to hold press conferences or issue press releases daily or even more often, but once the dust has settled, quiet down your activity. If there is no news to announce, many reporters will move on to the next story.

KEY POINTS

➤ Avoid crises by developing a crisis plan and convening a Crisis Committee.

➤ Remember to review and amend company policies, demonstrate humility, and avoid conflicts of interest.

➤ Look out for potential crises from within your ranks, develop policies for preventing crises.

➤ Avoid conflicts of interest and make sure your financial practices are unambiguous.

➤ Make sure your spokesperson is someone the press would deem trustworthy.

➤ If your company has bad news, you should be the one to announce it, rather than having it announced for you.

➤ When a crisis hits your company, protect it by acknowledging the problem and seeking legal and public relations counsel as needed.

➤ Try to see the opportunity in every crisis for articulating your Key Message Points.

HOMEWORK

➤ Form a Crisis Committee and schedule the committee's first preparedness meeting. At that first meeting, select a chairperson and hand out assignments with strict deadlines. Schedule future meetings and give them priority.

➤ Make every best effort not to cancel a crisis meeting. Your goal should be to have a complete crisis plan within three months.

How to Write and Review a Press Release

Lesson Plan

In this chapter, we introduce the basic formula for writing a stellar press release. We also discuss keeping your press release schedule on track. Finally, you learn what headlines garner the best coverage for your company.

This much is certain in business PR: There will come a time when you'll need to write your own press release. Perhaps your company is just starting out, and you haven't yet budgeted for a public relations professional. Or perhaps you're reviewing your past publicity efforts and trying to identify ways to strengthen this important medium for communicating with the press. In this chapter, you learn the basic rules for responding to the press, quickly and effectively, in writing.

There is no such thing as *writer's block* when it comes to writing a press release—there just isn't time for it.

A press release is news, and news has an essential time component. Therefore, when a press release for your company is in order, you need to move quickly. The entire process, from writing the first draft and securing reviews and edits to the actual release of the press release, should take no longer than three days.

The schedule goes like this:

- *Day 1:* Public relations person writes first draft of the press release and sends it to the company's officers, along with an e-mail that asks for them to respond with their edits by 10 A.M. the next business day.

- *Day 2:* If any company officer doesn't respond to the call for edits, the public relations person tracks him down and solicits, at the least, his verbal comments. By close of business, the public relations person has sent a new draft to company officers, as well as to the company's attorney. Any edits are due back first thing the following morning.

- *Day 3:* A final press release is composed incorporating the edits and presented to the officers, along with an e-mail informing them of when the release will be issued publicly. This e-mail should inform everyone of the *final* moment they can make changes.

See how quick that is? You don't have time for fancy writing tricks. Furthermore, a press release is no place for creative writing, excessive praise, or sales hype. The tone you should strive to achieve is one of fact-based professionalism that provides a straightforward accounting of the news.

As an example, which of the following lead paragraphs for a press release would you pick:

- As a barefoot boy in rural Mississippi, John Q. Public used to sit by the riverbanks and dream of owning a shipping line. The dream came true on Tuesday, when Company XYZ announced that it has rewarded Mr. Public's vision and commitment by appointing him CEO.
- Company XYZ, a leading shipbuilder, announced today that Abby Hannah is stepping down as chief executive officer of the company, but will stay on as chairman of the board. John Q. Public, currently the company's chief financial officer, will take over as CEO. Mr. Public has been with the company since 1995.

The first lead sounds like it is trying too hard to be a magazine profile. The second lead is informative and nonemotional. It's going to give potential investors, bankers, customers, and employees the most assurance that the company is handling a major change in its leadership without missing a beat.

The overall tone to strive for with your press release is professionalism. A press release is not an ad or a feature article; it's a record of the facts.

The Basics of Writing a Press Release

How do you figure out how to put those facts together? The best way to learn how to write a press release is to research how other companies have written up their own news. All you need is Internet access and a good search engine.

Let's say you are a clothing manufacturer and you want to write a press release about the company's new designs for the upcoming season. Open your Internet browser and do a search for "clothing manufacturers." The more specific you can be the better, so if your company manufactures baby clothes, then search for "infant clothing manufacturers" or "baby clothing manufacturers" or another broad term. The search will turn up hundreds, if not thousands, of web sites, and that is when your real research begins.

Click on each web site and look for the section of the site called "Press Information" or "Media Center" or "Recent Press Releases." Within an hour, you will have several press releases to use as models for the news you would like to put in your own news release.

Using the press release you found as a template, or guide, write your release. Start with the *headline*, which is the most important part of a press release. Many reporters, editors, and producers often have no time to read beyond the headline. Grab their attention by stating the company's essential news as one clear fact. For example, for the clothing manufacturing company mentioned above, a headline might be *Funky Baby Clothing Debuts Spring Line at New York Fashion Week Show.*

Another advantage to writing a great headline is that business people who sign up for business news e-mail services automatically receive news about certain industries or businesses or transactions. If any of those keywords appear in your news release, the release will show up in the databases to which they have subscribed.

Next comes the *subheadline*, which I believe is even more important than the primary headline because it allows a little more freedom for promotion. For example, *Funky Baby Clothing Featured in March in Style Magazine; Macy's, Saks to Carry Entire Line.*

One reason why this headline works is because it contains the names of large companies. Whenever you can put a big company's name in the headline, it confers a measure of credibility to your company.

Throughout the release, choose strong verbs and action words to tell your company's story. Instead of saying "inaugurated," try "launched." Instead of "has" or "are," try to find an appropriate action verb.

The one exception to this guideline is the word "said," which is preferable to any variation, including "stated," "chortled," "laughed," "intoned," "murmured," "went on," and so on; always stick with "said."

After you write the headline, use the following road map to build your press release:

Paragraph 1: State the news.

Paragraph 2: Explain the impact of the news.

Paragraph 3: A quote from the company's top executive.

Paragraph 4: Recent background about the company that relates to the news being announced.

Paragraph 5: A secondary quote, if needed.

Paragraph 6: Boilerplate information about the company.

Final Paragraph: If your company is a publicly traded company, you will need to insert the standard *Blue Sky* paragraph that warns against forward-looking statements and cautions investors about the risks. In the sample press release that is reprinted on the next page, the Blue Sky paragraph is at the end of the release, under the heading of "Forward-Looking Statements."

Depending on the news you want to announce, the road map might need to be tweaked here and there. But it is a good tool to use to get you to a first draft.

The actual press release that I have footnoted to help you see the road map in action starts on page 181.

Contact: Sally Stewart
555.555.5555
sally.stewart@mediatraining101.com[a]

National Lampoon Network Launches First TV Season[b]
TV Network Airs 12 Hours of Original Programming Each Week,
Reaches 3.5 Million College Students on 420 Campuses[c]

Los Angeles, CA, January 23, 2003[d]—National Lampoon (OTC BB: NLPN)[e] announced today that the comedy powerhouse has launched a new TV network that reaches 3.5 million college students on 420 American campuses. National Lampoon Network airs four hours of original programming three times a week, featuring shows that appeal to the network's core 18-to-24-year-old demographic.

National Lampoon Network is available to nearly one in four U.S. college students ages 18 to 24. Viewers who tune into The National Lampoon Network can watch shows, including:

- *Bridget the Midget:* A reality series that follows the exploits and challenges of Bridget, a sexy, 3'10" tall actress and rock singer.

- *Riffage Live:* A backstage interview show featuring up-and-coming rock bands as they perform live around the country, hosted by Bijou Phillips.

- *Gamers:* A review show in which two video game junkies, Matt Jones and Trish Suhr, critique new video games.

- *A/V Squad:* A cutting edge interview and live performance show hosted by Lesley Swanson. Recent appearances include Kid Rock, Tenacious D, Barenaked Ladies, and John Mayer.

---

[a] The name, phone number, and e-mail address of the company PR person. This should not be the CEO, and it should be someone who is easily reachable.
[b] Active words and a well-recognized brand name are helpful to any headline.
[c] The subhead explains the impact of the headline.
[d] The dateline is the city where the company is based, followed by the date the news was released.
[e] Include ticker symbols for any company that is publicly traded.

- *Half Baked*: A cooking show that explores the cuisine of music, sports, fashion, and acting icons, including Shaquille O'Neal with his morning omelet, Andy Roddick with "rock" potatoes, and Lisa Loeb with Texas Banana Cream Pie.
- *National Lampoon News*: A news show, hosted by comedian Ben Gleiberman, who puts National Lampoon's special spin on current events.

"National Lampoon Network's first slate of programming shows the company's potential to produce and deliver the kind of cutting-edge entertainment that 18-to-24-year-olds are tuning into today," said Doug Bennett, National Lampoon Executive Vice President. "For 30 years, National Lampoon has been an institution in college life, and now our TV network is going to carry on that tradition."[f]

National Lampoon Network launched its spring season on Jan. 17. "The minute we went on the air, our phones started ringing off the hook," Mr. Bennett said. "College students are excited that National Lampoon is on their campus and part of their college experience."

In 2002, National Lampoon acquired the assets of Burly Bear Network, one of the two major on-campus college television networks. The purchase included the television network, which is distributed exclusively to colleges and universities, as well as a library of top-rated college programming targeted directly at the 18-to-24-year-old demographic.[g]

National Lampoon is and has been one of the leading brands in comedy for the past 30 years. Today, National Lampoon is active in a broad array of entertainment activities, including feature films, television programming, interactive entertainment, home video, comedy audio CDs, and book publishing.[h]

---

[f] The quote should be factual about why the news is helpful to the company's goals.
[g] Recent background.
[h] This begins the boilerplate paragraphs that contain deeper background information about the company, and is included in every company news release. Boilerplate information often does not need to be changed more than once every six months.

In the 1970s and 1980s, *National Lampoon* was the most widely read publication on college campuses, while today, the web site, www.nationallampoon.com, is one of the most popular humor sites on the Internet.

The company also owns interests in all major National Lampoon properties, including *National Lampoon's Animal House*, the *National Lampoon Vacation* film series, and *National Lampoon's Van Wilder*.

This press release contains forward-looking statements that are based on the Company's current expectations, forecasts, and assumptions. In some cases forward-looking statements may be identified by forward-looking words like "would," "intend," "hope," "will," "may," "should," "expect," "anticipate," "believe," "estimate," "predict," "continue," or similar words.

Forward-looking statements involve risks and uncertainties, which could cause actual outcomes and results to differ materially from the company's expectations, forecasts, and assumptions. These risks and uncertainties include risks and uncertainties not in the control of the company, including, without limitation, the current economic climate in the United States and other risks and uncertainties, including those enumerated and described in the company's filings with the Securities and Exchange Commission, which filings are available on the SEC's web site at www.sec.gov. The company disclaims any intention or obligation to update or revise any forward-looking statements, whether as a result of new information, future events, or otherwise.

KEY POINTS

When writing a press release, make sure you:

➤ Use strong verbs and action words.
➤ State the news simply.

(continued)

KEY POINTS *(Continued)*

➤ Pay extra attention to the headline.

➤ Use quotes sparingly and strategically.

➤ Include background information on the company.

➤ Provide contact information.

HOMEWORK

➤ Take an old press release and edit it, using the principles outlined in this chapter.

How to Pitch Your Company's Story

Lesson Plan

Now that you know what makes for a good press release, we discuss the topic of how to interest reporters in doing a story on your company called pitching. *We outline the Seven Positive Pitching Actions.*

Pitching a story can be challenging, but the reward is potentially great press coverage. The first thing to know about pitching a story is that many senior public relations professionals rarely, if ever, pick up the phone to pitch a story to a reporter. In many large public relations agencies, pitching is left to the junior staff simply because it is widely considered to be the most odious task. After all, nobody likes rejection.

The fact is rejection is the result of story pitching the majority of the time. Even when you are an experienced story pitcher, you hear "no" frequently. However, in this chapter, I outline Seven Positive Pitching Actions that minimize rejection by giving reporters your information how and when they want it. Before starting on these principles, you need to decide if you are pitching an exclusive story or a news release. There is a difference.

Pitching a News Release

The advantage of choosing to make your announcement a news release is that you can control the precise timing. When you issue a news release on a paid wire service, such as BusinessWire or PR Newswire, you select the day your news will be released as well as the time.

The timing of a news release is an important consideration. Generally, it is a good idea to avoid issuing news releases on Mondays and Fridays. Mondays are usually crowded with important business news that has come to light throughout the weekend. Mondays are also when many major companies announce significant transactions, such as mergers and acquisitions. If your release can't compete with that news, it is much better to hold it for another day rather than risk attracting little or no attention. On Fridays, press releases don't get a lot of attention because this is when reporters are usually desperately trying to wrap up their stories for the week, especially if they are working on a Sunday newspaper story.

I suggest issuing the release on a paid wire service first thing on a business day, because reporters and editors who scan those releases, looking for stories and trends, start working pretty early, and you want to make sure your release catches their notice. When a company has news that is unpleasant, some public relations people will suggest releasing the news at 6 P.M. on a Friday. This tactic generally assures that the news will get little notice, but if you choose this route, be careful because it can backfire. Reporters who notice the release may think issuing the news at such an off-time is an indication that the company is trying to pull a fast one. Arousing any reporter's suspicion like this can easily lead to negative coverage. For example, when the Securities and Exchange Commission (SEC) executive appointed by President Bush decided to resign, the release went out late on a Friday afternoon. The SEC executive had been under intense media scrutiny for months. Pundits were calling for his resignation, editorials were criticizing his background and lackluster track record. Releasing the news at a time when the majority of reporters weren't paying attention guaranteed that the one reporter who was paying attention had a bigger story, and part of that story was the fact that the executive was trying to sneak this development past the Fourth Estate. As a result, reporters jumped on the story.

Pitching an Exclusive Story

Before you even select the time for your release, carefully consider whether you need a release at all. Not every story pitch needs one. Sometimes, especially when you are aiming for a feature story, a trend story, or a profile of a major executive, it is better to pitch to targeted reporters one at a time. If you have a good story, write a brief—no longer than one computer screen of text—pitch memo and e-mail it to the reporter of your choice. A day or two later, follow up with a phone call. Make sure you tell him that you might issue a press release, but you wanted to make sure that he had a chance to decide if he wanted to break the story.

Reporters always want to be the first to report a story—make sure they understand they have that option with the story you are pitching them.

Once you have determined if your story is going to be a press release or a one-by-one pitch, then you are ready to integrate the Seven Positive Pitching Actions into your pitching style.

The Seven Positive Pitching Actions

1. Think beyond your own news.
2. Target the right reporters.
3. State the facts.
4. Time it right.
5. Offer photos, charts, samples, and other resources.
6. Follow up.
7. Get excited.

1. *Think beyond your own news.* Reporters usually don't say no to story pitches just because they don't want to do the work or make the investment in time and reporting energy. Reporters say no because the story idea isn't interesting, isn't on their beat, or isn't newsworthy in their opinion.

For example, if I call a reporter at *Investor's Business Daily* and offer him an opportunity to break a story on a CPA practice in Indianapolis that has just been sold for $75,000, this pitch is going to land flat. First, the amount of money changing hands is so small—compared to the mega-deals that *Investor's Business Daily* regularly covers—that a reporter for a top-tier financial paper is not going to be interested.

What if the pitch about the CPA practice in Indianapolis includes the fact that this is one of 15 or 20 such purchases by a major accounting firm? This angle could get a reporter's attention because it suggests a major business shift on the part of the accounting industry.

A single development might not interest a reporter, but a series of similar developments could illustrate that your news is part of a sea change in business or a significant shift in a particular industry or economic sector.

Another way to think beyond the borders of your own news is to think of your news within the context of emerging trends. When I was a reporter at *USA Today,* we had a saying: Three makes a trend. If you could identify three isolated, but similar incidents, then you could write a story about how a certain trend was hot. For example, take something as simple as the color yellow. If a major company changes the color of their logo to yellow and home improvement stores note an increase in sales of yellow paint, then all it will take is for a major television star to be photographed driving a yellow car before a lifestyle reporter does a story about how the color yellow is the hot color of the moment. *People* magazine covers trends on a regular basis. In 2002, one of that magazine's most popular cover stories was about famous women who celebrated their curvy figures and who weren't trying to diet themselves into a size zero. They saw this as a trend.

2. *Target the right reporters.* Once you have honed your story and backed it up with a big-picture angle, then turn your attention to your media list. When I was a reporter, it always shocked me when I would get calls from public relations professionals who obviously didn't give any thought as to whether I would be interested in their story. For example, they would pick up the phone and call to pitch me on attending a press conference at an amusement park that was unveiling a new merry-go-round. Even though I can see the potential for this story as a viable, fun lifestyle piece, it wasn't my beat; I covered hard news. Political races, earthquakes, mudslides, plane crashes, murder trials. My editors weren't interested in me spending a day at an amusement park when there was a wildfire burning out of control in Malibu.

Many public relations people create pages and pages of media lists, without even considering whether the reporters on the list would be the slightest bit interested in the story they are pitching. Without that consideration and thoughtfulness, those media lists are virtually worthless. The bottom line is that you have to target the right reporters, otherwise all you'll have to show for your pitching is a big phone bill.

To target the right reporters, the public relations person needs to consume a lot of media. I am always shocked when I walk into a public relations agency and see that the only televisions in the entire office are in the general manager's office and the conference room. The people who are charged with pitching stories on a daily basis never even watch the television programs that they are pitching. How would they ever know whether the company they are working with is a good candidate for a *Today Show* piece if they don't know that the *Today Show* is doing a series of stories on the very industry that company represents?

Media consumption must go beyond television watching, if you want to be a successful pitcher. You have to read newspapers, magazines, annual reports, supermarket tabloids, weekly neighborhood newspapers, web sites, Dear Abby—anything that gives a clear snapshot of the mood of society. Every couple of weeks, a successful pitcher goes to a newsstand and picks up the publications with which their clients would best fit. In addition, the successful pitcher throws in a couple of publications that are off the beaten path. They understand the idea that you never know which publication will spark a story idea, so they look for ideas everywhere.

By consuming a lot of media, a pitcher begins to develop a sense of which reporters are interested in which stories. They'll be able to target their pitches to the reporters who have actually demonstrated that they are interested in covering the story they are pitching.

3. *State the facts.* When I need to pitch a story, I usually start by composing an e-mail that I will send to reporters one by one. Each e-mail states the facts of the story I am proposing, offers a larger context for the news development, and demonstrates that I am familiar with their publication or their own work. Finally, I make sure that no reporter ever has to work to figure out how to get in touch with me.

A day or so later, I print out the e-mail and have a copy of the company's press release in hand before I call to check in with the reporter. If I get the reporter's voice mail, I generally hang up without leaving a message because the last call a reporter will return is a pitch call from a public relations executive. Reporters rarely call

Here's a sample of an e-mail that I might send:

Hi Joe,

I have noticed you have been covering quite a few business developments in the weight loss industry and wanted to make sure you were aware of Company ABC's new product, Skinny4Ever, which is a chocolate milkshake that melts fat and pounds within 30 minutes of ingestion. Skinny4Ever was invented by University Medical School professor Jill Jones, MD, and has just been approved by the Food and Drug Administration. The FDA recently has approved a dozen new weight loss products, so perhaps you might be interested in doing a round-up of the various new choices soon available for overweight Americans. I'll check in with you in a few days to see if you are interested in interviewing Dr. Jones. In the meantime, you can contact me at 555.555.5555 or via e-mail at sally.stewart@mediatraining101.com. Below my signature, I am cutting and pasting a copy of the press release Company ABC issued today.

Sally Stewart

back a flack. (When you don't get a call returned, then you have to call again, which only lets the reporter think that you are a nuisance. I'd rather just try again later.)

If the reporter answers the phone, I don't waste any time. I quickly state my name and say that I recently sent him intriguing news about Company ABC and I thought he would be interested in the development because he has been covering that general issue. Sometimes, the reporter will ask a few questions and I might need to consult my fact sheet or press release, both of which are right there in front of me.

Sometimes, the reporter will ask for additional information, which I often use as an opportunity to say that the company president would be available for a quick get-to-know conversation because she is the best person to provide that additional information.

Sometimes, the reporter will say that he'll think about it and let me know. That is when I make a note on my calendar to check in with him in a few days. Sometimes, he will tell me flat-out that he isn't interested, and occasionally, everything comes together and the reporter wants to do the story.

If the reporter turns me down, I might ask if he thinks any other reporter at their outlet might be interested and, if possible, I get that reporter's name and number. Then I quickly say thanks and move on to the next target.

There is a reporter for every story. It might not be the reporter or the publication that you would dream of enticing, but there will be a reporter somewhere who is interested.

Resist the impulse to push a reporter who is declining. It's important to build a strong relationship with each reporter because you'll surely have a reason to call him again for another story. When you call back later, the reporter will remember that you were pleasant and he'll then listen to your new pitch. I have successfully pitched several stories that way.

Too, as we discussed in Chapter 1, reporters who are badgered into doing a story generally produce a story you aren't going to be thrilled with. Also, if they turn you down and you nag and beg and protest, they will immediately put you into the nuisance category and hang up as quickly as possible.

4. *Time it right.* I never make calls to reporters without paying attention to this fourth Positive Pitching Action. The timing of your pitch is a crucial consideration.

For example, if you are going to pitch a story on a specific day, but a major national news event unfolds that very morning, then you should probably rethink your schedule.

When you know that every available reporter and editor is swamped with covering a major news event, don't pitch a story that will be just as fresh a week from now.

Once, in the midst of the O. J. Simpson murder trial, I got a call from a public relations person seeking coverage about a social trend that I actually would have wanted to cover: the exponential increase in the number of foster children. But the O. J. story was my beat and there was no time for anything else.

"I am so sick of reporters telling me that they are too swamped on O. J.!" the clearly exasperated public relations person said.

The truth is that I was sick of it, too. But I was on a deadline, and my only suggestion for him was to write a letter to the editor.

5. *Offer photos, charts, samples, and other resources.* Reporters, particularly those at smaller or trade publications, are always on the lookout for photos and other graphic elements to accompany their stories. Don't make them work too hard to come up with the art they need. Tell a reporter that you have a chart that illustrates the poll results in your press release. Let a reporter know that you can e-mail him a photograph of the CEO.

For example, one of my clients, a nonprofit organization, wanted to get some coverage of their annual crime-fighting day. National

---

Tips for Calling Reporters

- Daily newspaper reporters are generally swamped after 3:30 P.M., working on their story for the next day's paper. Unless you are call-ing to help them with that story, you should wait.

- Two hours before a television news program goes on the air, pro-ducers are feverishly attending to last-minute details.

- Monday, Tuesday, and Wednesday are generally good days to call a weekly magazine or weekly trade newspaper.

- At five-day-a-week newspapers like *Investor's Business Daily, The Wall Street Journal*, and *USA Today*, many reporters don't work on Fridays because they work on Sundays. Try calling them on Sun-day, when nobody else is trying to get them on the phone.

- You can further capitalize on your good timing by opening your phone call with the question, "Are you on deadline?" Often, re-porters appreciate it when a public relations person is considerate enough to ask. That is no guarantee that they will do your story, but at least they will be more amenable to listening to your pitch.

coverage was crucial because Congress was scheduled to vote on their appropriation in a couple of weeks. I told the client that we needed to put together a chart that outlined their crime-fighting day activities in a variety of cities and towns across the country. When I called to pitch their first-choice newspaper, the fact that I had already compiled a chart made the reporter's day. The story ran with the chart and my client was thrilled.

Another reason to provide the art for the story is that you can exercise more control over the story. For example, you can ensure that the story runs a flattering photo of your CEO. You might also suggest other sources that are not officially aligned with your client or company. If, for example, your pitch is about a new antivirus software, you might want to tell a reporter about an independent study of antivirus software in which your client was highly rated.

6. *Follow up.* But be smart about it. To a reporter, there are few questions more annoying than: Did you get the fax? For one thing, it immediately signals that this is a call from a public relations professional, and most reporters will then hurry to conclude the phone call. For another, if the reporter is interested, then he will call.

I try to avoid sending faxes in the first place. Most reporters don't have their own fax machines and the faxes end up all muddled together in the mailroom unless a vigilant mailroom employee makes sure they are delivered. I prefer to send an e-mail, which is nearly guaranteed to show up in front of the reporter's very own eyes.

Still, following up is critical to getting the story you want. If you promise to send a photo, do it immediately if not sooner. If you say that you have put together information for a chart, then make sure you send it ASAP. If you send information, but don't hear back from the reporter, call them to quickly check in—but keep the conversation short and to the point.

7. *Get excited.* This is probably the most important Positive Pitching Action. On days I know I am going to be pitching, I drive to work with my stereo blasting some music that is going to pump

me up, energize me, help put me in a positive frame of mind so that rejection won't get in my way. I let the music set a positive mood and that helps me feel confident.

Confidence Is the Key to a Good Pitch

Remember what we learned about the "yes, but" frame of mind that many reporters exhibit—this attitude is often a negative one. You need to feel incredibly confident whenever you talk to a journalist, because only then will you be able to communicate with him as a peer. If a reporter senses that you are weak and unsure, the conversation isn't going anywhere.

One way to boost your confidence is to boost your energy level. Whenever I spend a day working the phones, pitching a story, I wear a telephone headset with an extra long cord so I can stand up and walk around my office while I pitch. During the pitch, I might make an occasional joke or otherwise demonstrate that I have a personality, but I remind myself that a little bit goes a long way. Finally, I avoid sounding too much like a sales pitch, because this is a major turnoff to reporters. Remember, reporters went into the reporting business because they wanted to communicate with the world and make it a better place by righting the wrongs. They don't want to give you a free ad. Sound like a member of the sales team and you could talk a reporter *out* of doing a story.

When you do talk, pay attention to the tone of your voice. If your voice rises at the end of every sentence, as it does when you ask a question, it makes you sound tentative and childlike at a time when you want to sound like you have the greatest story in the world.

Even if you do have the best story in the world, brace yourself for a little rough treatment. Some reporters have a general dislike for public relations people and if they are in a poor mood at the moment you call, you are going to feel their hostility. If they are in a rush or on deadline, they will just want to end the call as soon as possible and they won't be gentle or try to spare your feelings.

I have actually heard reporters say to public relations people, "I never take news from flacks" and then hang up. Even when I was a reporter, I didn't understand that way of thinking—after all, reporters are supposed to have their fingers on the pulse of what is happening in their corner of the world. Not every story pitched by a public relations professional is going to be page one material, but it is also quite possible that it is not garbage, either. Listening to a story pitch isn't going to compromise a reporter's integrity; they might even learn something that might be interesting to their readers, listeners, or viewers.

If they don't see it that way, though, there is little you can do about it. Reread the Seven Positive Pitching Points and dial the next name on your media list.

KEY POINTS

The Seven Positive Pitching Actions:

1. Think beyond your own news.
2. Target the right reporters.
3. State the facts.
4. Time it right.
5. Offer photos, charts, samples, and other resources.
6. Follow up.
7. Get excited.

HOMEWORK

➤ Write a pitch memo about your company.

CHAPTER

18

How to Hire
PR That Works

Lesson Plan

*Both internal and external public relations (PR) programs
come with their unique pluses and minuses. In this chapter, we
discuss how you can determine which path is right for your
company. I include the questions to ask consultants and yourself before embarking on a PR program.*

There is a real difference between quality public relations and
the hype that went on before the stock market bubble burst.
Back then, everybody wanted to invest money to start and
expand new companies—especially those that had a smidgen of
high-tech in their product line. Money was so plentiful that companies could spend large amounts on their public relations activities. Many CEOs thought that public relations was a good way to
keep the investment money pouring into their companies because

venture capitalists would read their latest news release and get swept up in the excitement. They were right. The money kept coming and PR agencies found themselves swamped with more business than they could handle.

The effect of all this on PR agencies was that agency leaders couldn't find enough talented practitioners to do the work. At the same time, entrepreneurial companies were so convinced that they needed to hire a PR agency to spread their message that they were willing to pay top dollar.

I have heard many stories from CEOs who believe that they were burned by PR agencies. They say they were promised that their company would get onto the front page of *The New York Times*. Six months later, all the CEOs have to show for their money is a yellowing strategic public relations plan, two press releases, and a story in the local business journal. To add insult to injury, the CEOs tell me, the agency leaders didn't seem to care about the meager results. Back when venture capital was flowing, there was a long line of desperate clients waiting for a PR agency to do them the favor of taking their money.

Indeed, during that boom period, PR agencies increased their fees to the point that when a former director of communications for a web site design company I know went in search of an agency, she was told by each agency she contacted in New York and Los Angeles that unless she could spend $25,000 a month, for a minimum of six months, they didn't want her business. They wouldn't even make the time to meet with her. It sounds incredible now, but back then, a few agencies had outgoing voice mail messages on their phone lines that informed callers that they were not accepting new clients at this time.

Some companies did, indeed, get quality public relations. But many more just got a big bill and a couple of small clips.

When the recession first hit in 2001, many company leaders had to face the fact that they needed to get their spending under control. Often, in that situation, the first line item to be cut was the public relations budget. However, after a few years without public relations, many companies have found that they have no way of regularly informing investors, business partners, employees, and customers about their milestones, growth, and products and services. To boot, the relationships the CEO had fostered with reporters and editors have since grown stale.

The good news is that when the influx of new clients began drying up, many agencies began actively campaigning for smaller accounts and touting their performance records. Still, buyer-beware attitude is essential before you hire a PR firm, and it's crucial to do your homework.

Determine If You Want to Outsource Public Relations or Develop It In-House

The first question you need to tackle is whether your company would most benefit from hiring an outside agency or whether you want to bring your public relations initiative in-house.

An outside firm makes sense if you cannot afford to hire a full-time employee or if your public relations department is already working at capacity and needs extra help with specific projects. Fees for these services range from a few hundred a month to more than $50,000 a month, depending on the scope of work. Whatever the price tag, you need to know what you are getting for your money.

Hands down, the most important quality to look for is whether the consultant you are thinking of hiring has any journalism experience. I am sure many PR agency managers will disagree with me, but I stand firm in my belief that it is easier for a journalist to learn how to recognize good public relations than it is for a PR person to learn how to recognize good journalism. In fact, there are several PR agencies that hire former journalists exclusively. Other relevant non-agency experience includes working on a political campaign or for an elected official because politics is so reliant on communicating through journalists to the public. Finally, if your prospective PR person has been an attorney who worked on high-profile cases or has significant financial services experience—perhaps as an analyst—their experience will help your company, too. The bottom line is that you want someone working on your public relations who has worked with the media from more than one angle.

The inside story on PR agency life is that agencies are full of employees whose first job right out of school is as an assistant account executive at a large PR firm, where they spend their days photocopying, putting together media lists, answering the phone, and doing Internet research. They have stayed on the agency side for so long that they lose sight of the bigger media picture. As a result, they know how a PR agency operates, but little or nothing about how journalism works. The only way to learn about journalism is to spend some time in a newsroom. Sit in on editorial story meetings. Actually experience what it is like to be on deadline and get a call from a public relations professional who is pushing a story that isn't on your beat but still won't take no for an answer.

A PR person who has logged some time being immersed in the culture of a newsroom knows how journalists think and, therefore, understands how to best communicate your company in a way that compels journalists to find out more.

Of course there are rare exceptions, but in general, public relations people who have never spent even just one college summer internship in a newsroom have no firsthand, inside knowledge of how the media actually works.

Questions to Ask before Making a Hiring Decision

After you have determined whether the public relations person you are considering has a news background, ask yourself the following questions before rushing into a contract for PR services.

Who Is Going to Be Working on My Account?

Many large agencies send two senior consultants on the new business pitch, but when the work begins, it is often handed to junior
staff members who have little experience. The senior consultants
are not involved in the day-to-day work; they merely give their junior staff members' work a quick edit before they slap their own name
on it and send it to the client. Some large agencies will swear to you
that they don't do a "bait and switch" like that, but ask for specifics.

Ask for an approximate number of hours the senior consultants
will be devoting to your account monthly. Ask how many other accounts they are supervising.

It is a dirty little secret in big PR agencies that the higher you
climb up the agency ladder, the less you actually pitch stories.
Senior-level public relations professionals who actually work in
media relations are rare, but look and you'll find one.

Do I Really Need a Big Firm?

If yours is a multinational company with offices—and public relations issues—around the globe, then the answer is probably yes. But
if yours is a small company, you can probably find a public relations
freelancer or a boutique firm that can do a great job for you at about
30 to 50 percent of the cost of hiring a big agency. If you need help
locating firms, ask your business contacts or contact the Public Relations Society of America (www.prsa.org) and ask for referrals.

What Is the Hiring Process Like?

Call and set up a meeting with a public relations professional. The
initial consultation is usually free. Ideally, the meeting will take place
at your place of business so the public relations people can begin to
get a feel for your company.

At the meeting, everyone should introduce himself or herself,
talking for about two minutes about their role in the company.

State your specific goals for your business and why you are seeking public relations at this time. Perhaps your goal could be that you are opening a store and want consumers to know about it. Or maybe you are thinking of selling your business a few years from now and would like to begin to maximize the value of your brand. Alternatively, your company might be reaching out to a new audience.

Following this meeting, the public relations professional should write a short memo spelling out the kind of public relations program they can offer you. If you like the memo, you can meet again to hammer out basic terms. Unless yours is a big-bucks account, asking for more than two meetings with a public relations professional—who isn't billing for his initial meeting(s), after all—approaches the excessive mark.

How Should You Be Billed for the Work?

Should you choose to pay according to hours billed to your account? Or should you agree to a monthly retainer? My advice is that it is most cost-effective for the client to pay a monthly retainer, which is arrived at by the agency estimating how many hours it will take them to do the work for you every month. Most months, you will probably get a better deal than if you paid for each billable hour. Always ask for your bill to itemize the hours worked and what work was done during those hours.

How Much Should You Pay?

Again, it all depends on the amount of hours and the public relations person's billable rate. Today, at many large firms, a junior person's billable hour rate is around $85, while a senior level PR pro bills anywhere from $275 up. But from the moment your initial consultation begins, you should be open about your budget. You don't need to commit to a specific dollar amount until you are ready to sign the contract, but give a range of the level of public relations program you want. Don't get recommendations for pro-grams you cannot afford.

Can They Keep Their Promises?

If any public relations professional tells you that they can guarantee placing any story—I don't care what it is—they are out of their minds. I always tell prospective clients that I think their story is in-teresting and I will try to get it into *The Wall Street Journal* but there is one little hurdle: *The Wall Street Journal* has not yet named me front page editor, so I can't promise anything but my best ef-forts. Besides, once I get immersed in the company, it might be that their story is better suited to another publication.

What Is This Success Clause in the Contract?

Some agencies actually request a *success fee* meaning that they get a bonus if their work results in a major positive article or television segment about your company. The first time I heard about a success clause I was shocked. Nevertheless, the practice has become more common.

What Is the Scope of Work?

The first thing any public relations professional will want to do after you sign a contract—most firms will want a three- or six-month agreement—is write a strategic plan. Read it over and make any changes you want. The firm should be able to deliver the plan to you within 5 days of beginning work on your account.

Once you have approved the document, let this be your plan for at least six months to a year. I have worked at three PR agencies and I know that some public relations people write plans the way lawyers write letters. Believe me—you don't need that many strategic plans.

In addition, be wary of public relations folks who suggest doing everything but media. They might suggest a five-year plan or a crisis plan. They might want to schedule a number of conference calls, and they might tell you that they'll evaluate your customer relations department, but if they don't mention doing media work, then move on.

What Is My Role?

Public relations does not work in a vacuum. There is no way a public relations person—even the best of the best—can walk into your company and immediately intuit every aspect of your business. Especially at the beginning of your agency relationship, someone at your company needs to be available to answer questions immediately as they come up. Someone has to make sure the agency gets copies of the company brochures and knows about upcoming trade shows. Someone has to be able to schedule executives for key meetings. Your biggest responsibility is to make sure the lines of communication are wide open.

How Will I Know It Is Working?

Do not expect results the next day. It takes several weeks for a public relations professional to develop a customized plan for your business and to target reporters who would be interested in covering your story. It takes time for each reporter to become interested enough to pitch their editor on doing the story. Once the editor agrees, the reporter—and the story—swiftly moves through the reporting, editing, and publishing processes.

Regardless of whether you decide to hire an outside agency or hire a full-time employee, you need to give your public relations plan time to work. Getting a story or putting out a press release always takes longer that you think it will. You need to be working on multiple stories at the same time to build up your pipeline of results. That does not mean that the PR office is quiet during that time. It takes media lists and phone calls and more phone calls and pitch memos and time to accomplish it. By the end of three months, if you have not seen any results from your public relations program, you should consider making a change.

Maximize Your In-House PR Personnel

Some of these questions can also help you define the role of an in-house PR person. However, before you commit to a new employee, make sure you are setting the stage for success. The following list will help you ensure that your internal public relations department is able to succeed.

Provide Support

Public Relations is time consuming. Do you want your public relations person to be collating press kit materials? You might, but if you can afford it, administrative support is key to success. Decide upfront the amount of resources you are able to commit to public relations. What is your budget for magazine subscriptions, media databases, networking meetings, lunches, and permission rights?

Keep Your PR Person in the Loop

If solid public relations is a key component of your company's success, then you need to make sure that your public relations professional is privy to company initiatives. Let him in on the planning stage. He might have some advice that will help nail a key story placement at the crucial moment.

Define the Job

I believe that public relations and marketing must be separate functions. The mind-sets that go with each discipline are so different that combining the two responsibilities is counterproductive. I have never seen a company that combined marketing and PR into one person's responsibilities—or even one department's domain—and found it to be a recipe for success.

Let Your PR Person Out

If he or she is in their office all day every day, something is wrong. Your public relations person needs to be out, meeting with re- porters, networking with the City Council, representing your com- pany at community functions.

Don't Expect a Yes Person

A good public relations professional says no sometimes or makes suggestions on how to better handle issues that arise. A confident public relations professional who is in control can tactfully suggest wearing a different tie or perhaps suggest adding a particular anec- dote to a speech. You want someone to help guide your public image, not a sycophant.

Following the guidelines in this chapter will help ensure that your public relations program brings results.

KEY POINTS

➤ Whether your company should establish an internal public rela- tions department or hire an agency of freelance public relations person is a decision only you can make.

➤ During your decision process, ask public relations professionals and your own staff the questions that will help you make the right decisions.

➤ Determine what you can afford to spend on public relations as well as the results you would like.

➤ Allow your new public relations program a few months to kick into full gear before scrutinizing the results.

➤ Give your public relations staff the necessary support for making them able to do their jobs well.

Homework

➤ Write your wish list. Which publications would you like to see cover your company? Be clear with your public relations person about your top priorities for coverage.

➤ Make another list, this one of all the documents that a public relations person will need to understand your company, such as corporate bios of senior executives, the most recent business plan, the company mission statement, and so on.

➤ Review several months' worth of trade publications that cover your industry and identify which companies appear to have the best coverage. Go to that company's web site and review their posted public relations materials, such as news releases.

How to Create a Stellar Press Kit

Lesson Plan

Having a great press kit on hand can help you to attract new media coverage. It is essential to have a press kit that's accessible and concise. This will ensure that people see your press kit as a resource, not a roadblock.

When I was a reporter, we had a special way of dealing with most corporate press kits. Most of them went into what we called the *Circular File*.

Every newsroom has a Circular File. Circular, as in, the mail carrier delivers the mail, a reporter—or maybe an intern—opens most of it, and the unsolicited glossy folders that look and read like sales kits get dumped in the newsroom trash bin, which is emptied nightly.

Of course, there were a few exceptions. We often kept the super-elaborate press kits, the ones that came in multicolored custom-made folders, often adorned with Velcro closures and other gizmos. We didn't keep them around as a reference tool; we kept them to show to our colleagues, other reporters and editors, so we could have a good laugh at companies for spending their money foolishly.

This chapter is designed to make sure that your company press kit makes it onto a reporter's desk instead of into the Circular File. It is a lot simpler than you think.

Make Your Press Kit Simple and Informative

A succinct, simple, well-constructed press kit is a company essential. It can be used for a variety of audiences. A press kit can be given to potential business partners as a leave-behind following an important meeting. Potential investors also find it useful. Even reporters keep it around—even consult it—but only if it is done right.

To that end, follow these rules when constructing your press kit:

1. Less is more.
2. Let 'em ask.
3. Make it lean.
4. Assemble with care.
5. Ask permission.
6. Shop carefully for freebies.
7. Go high tech.

Let's take the rules in detail.

Less Is More

For some reason, whenever business people hear the words *press kit,* they leap to the conclusion that it is going to cost them a lot of money. Nothing could be further from the truth. In the media world, when it comes to press kits, simple is better than fancy, and less is more. There is absolutely no reason to spend thousands of dollars only to end up with 1,000-plus press kits, most of which will just sit in their box in the closet, gathering dust and taking up space, as I'll mention in the next rule. All you need is a local office supply store and your computer printer and within a few days, your business, too, can have a press kit.

Most of the time, people go overboard with their press kit projects. One of my clients, a Hollywood entertainment company, hired me and at our first official work session, unveiled the press kit folders that they had spent hours designing. The folders were adorned with the company's logo as well as more than a dozen images from films and TV programs the company produced. There were so many graphics on the folder that you didn't know where to look first and the company's internationally recognized logo was lost in the clutter.

My first question: "How many of these folders did you have printed?"

The answer: "Only about 500."

Inwardly, I groaned. Outwardly, I instructed my client not to order any more and that I would design the next jacket. This time, the company's press kit folder would adhere to the Number-One rule of press kits: Less is more.

Making a great press kit is as simple as going to the neighborhood office supply store and buying a plain color glossy folder. (I am partial to the silver ones, but any solid color will do.)

While you're at the store, pick up a pack of labels with adhesive on the back. The labels have to be large enough to accommodate your company logo. Go back to your office and print your logo on the labels. Now here is the tricky part: When you stick the labels on the folder, place them on the bottom third of the folder. The place-ment of the logo is crucial because of the next rule.

Let 'Em Ask

It is not a good idea to send your press kits to reporters who didn't ask for it. Most of the time, it will go straight into the Circular File. Even if a reporter does save it and has every good intention of look-ing at it when he has a free moment, that free moment might never come. Every day, more and more mail gets piled on top of the press kit. Once every six months or so, when the reporter can't stand the mess anymore, he'll just throw away everything on his desk, includ-ing, of course, your press kit.

Instead of trying to entice a reporter with a press kit, get him interested in a specific news story about your company.

As we discussed in Chapter 18 on pitching a story, e-mail your story pitch, and maybe follow up with a phone call. Once you have interested him in what is going on with your company, he might re-quest more information or you can offer to send him your press kit.

If you're able to then meet with the reporter, you'll be glad that the logo is on the bottom third of the folder because you can write a handwritten note to the reporter and paperclip it to the top. The note shouldn't cover up the company logo, making for a subliminal, but powerful, presentation of the information.

The note itself doesn't need to be anything fancy. It simply says something like, "Hi Clark, I enjoyed our lunch today. Here is the press kit I promised. Call me at 555-5555 if you have any questions. Thanks, Sally."

That personal touch is what will set your press kit apart and encourage the reporter to scan its contents with a mind that is open to doing a story. The point is not to send out 500 press kits that end up in the Circular File; the point is to have a press kit available as a reference tool for people who are truly interested in learning more about your company.

Make It Lean

The contents of your press kit should be streamlined. If there is too much information, some reporters will be intimidated by the sheer amount of the reading material and give up before they even get started. All you need is the following:

- *The company overview:* A basic biography of the company, including date it was founded, company mission, description of products and services, and historic company events. The overview doesn't need to be longer than three pages, double-spaced. Take care that the overview is not overly boastful in tone, but rather states the facts about the company in a professional manner.

- *Senior management bios:* Short corporate biographies of the top company leaders or principals. Corporate bios should contain information about the principal's career, but little information about their private lives, including hobbies or family members.

- *Clips, clips, clips:* Reporters are usually skeptical of company brochures because they think they are so much braggadocio. However, reporters are rarely cynical about other reporters' stories. Reporters, like the rest of us, tend to think that if a story was published in a reputable publication, then the information is credible. Clips of stories about your company are the best information you can include in your press kit.

If you don't yet have any clips to include, you can include the following:

- *Recent press releases:* Include a couple of your recent press releases, but don't include press releases that are more than six months old. (Remember the principles you learned in Chapter 4, *What Is News?* Don't lose sight of the fact that reporters are interested in current news, not history.) In addition, press releases are more potent if they have been issued by one of the paid business newswire services, like PR Newswire or BusinessWire. It costs approximately $150 to purchase distribution in a major metropolitan area such as New York or Los Angeles. If your news release contains actual news, it will get "picked up," or reprinted, in an online publication or an industry trade magazine.

- *A brochure or catalogue:* Again, the simpler the better.
- *Photos:* Resist the urge to include photos that show a company officer giving an oversized check to a local charity. Instead, include a photo of a flagship retail outlet, a photo of company headquarters, or a shot of the CEO with the company's products.
- *Charts or lists:* You could include a list of products or company locations or major clients.

When assembling these materials, remember to use discretion. You don't want the press kit to be so weighted down that people feel like they'll never have the time to read it. Reporters will pass on taking any kits that appear cumbersome.

Assemble with Care

The assembly of your kit is important, and it should follow this order:

1. Company-generated information should go in the folder in the left-side pocket.
2. Clips of news stories featuring the company should go on the right side.
3. The first piece of paper on each side—the ones that come into view when the folder is opened—should be easy to read and well designed.

4. Company information should be topped with a company logo.

5. Put the clips in the order you want them read, generally with the most impressive clip on top. If you are debating whether to put the two-page feature from your local newspaper or the brief mention from *The Wall Street Journal* on the top of the pile, I would encourage you to go with *The Wall Street Journal*.

6. Buy the kind of folders that have notches inside for business cards. Put your public relations person's business card in the notches.

7. Overall, be careful to leave out any overtly "sales-pitch" material, such as price lists and order forms.

Ask Permission

It might be tempting, but don't Xerox copies of an article and put them in your press kit. Published stories are copyrighted. Photocopying them as you please without gaining permission from the publication amounts to nothing less than stealing. Your company does not need that kind of reputation, especially among the press itself.

Instead, contact the publication and ask for permission. Most newspapers have someone in charge of reprints and they will grant reprint permission for a small fee. Some prestigious magazines like *Forbes* charge a more substantial fee and require you to order reprints from them. If you bring the article to your own printer, then be sure to add "Reprinted With Permission" on the bottom of each clip.

Shop Carefully for Freebies

Freebies can be fun to a reporter, but they should not be too elaborate or disconnected from the company's products. For example, if yours is a telecom company, a good freebie might be a retractable phone/Internet cord. A dry cleaning company could send a logo'd lint-remover. Pens are always good because every reporter needs another to replace the one he just lost. Most of the stuff that comes in is just junk.

A friend of mine who is a Hollywood/entertainment reporter for a major publication says that the best freebie she ever got was the dozen long-stem multicolored roses Paramount Pictures sent to entertainment reporters to promote their Mel Gibson-Helen Hunt movie, *What Women Want,* when it first came out in theaters. This was a brilliant public relations move. Nobody—not even the most antifreebie reporter—is going to send the flowers back. At the most, they will give the flowers to a newsroom receptionist and everyone who stops by her desk is going to ask, "Where did those incredible flowers come from?" Newsroom buzz—isn't that what the movie studio wanted?

Whatever the freebie, make sure it's not worth more than a couple of dollars because most reporters will refuse to accept anything that looks like an attempt to buy positive coverage. One of my clients has a backyard vineyard and makes award-winning wine in a special winemaking room he built in his house. He wanted to give a bottle to a visiting reporter whom we knew had just recently been on a tour of vineyards in California. When we gave the reporter the bottle of wine, we took care to explain that it had no material value because my client was not legally allowed to sell his homemade wine.

Even following these guidelines, freebies like yet another key chain and memo pad end up in the box every newsroom has. The box is usually in the corner of the newsroom or in the lunchroom. It's where reporters throw the freebies they don't want. At *USA Today,* we'd wait until the box got filled up and then the office manager would load it into her car and drop it at the neighborhood Goodwill donation box.

Go High Tech

Anything that is available in your press kit should also be available in electronic form. This is easy enough to do, by setting up a page on your company's web site and calling it your "Press Center." Web site visitors can click on Press Center to call up recent press releases, annual reports, links to media stories, and so on. (See Chapter 20 for more information on public relations and the Internet.) You can also reproduce your press kit as a PDF file and e-mail it to reporters. You might also put the documents on a CD.

One thing to consider is that quite a few publications will not sell electronic rights to their stories. This has something to do with the fact that publications haven't yet unlocked the mystery of how to make a profit on electronic publishing, so they are loathe to give away those rights, even for a fee. Those publications generally will allow you to have a link on your web site that leads to their story on their web site.

KEY POINTS

➤ The bottom line is that you want your press kit to give just enough information without appearing overwhelming or boastful.

➤ Make your press kit lean, simple, and concise.

➤ Be sure to obtain permission before including any copyrighted material in your press kit.

➤ You want it to be credible and informative but easily understandable and not overly technical.

➤ Use discretion when selecting freebies.

➤ You certainly want your press kit to make it past the dreaded Circular File.

HOMEWORK

➤ Create and assemble the various components of a press kit, including past stories about the company, a company overview, or senior executive bios.

Media Training and the World Wide Web

Lesson Plan

A web site needs to be more than an electronic version of your company's brochure. In this chapter, we discuss how to update your site to help reporters. We also outline steps for writing your web site content so reporters will actually read it.

Whenever a potential new client calls me to see about working together, the first question I ask is, "What is your web site address?"

Then, as I type the address into my web browser, the client frequently apologizes for the state of the company's web site. "Our web site needs some work," the client might say. "We need to do a complete redesign, so don't hold it against us."

I don't hold an imperfect web site against them, but their customers and the media might. However, this is totally preventable.

Web site design is the business equivalent of working on your personal income tax return. It's something you know you have to do, but you keep putting it off and putting it off because it feels like it will take forever. When you finally do sit down and do it, you realize it doesn't take nearly as much time as you thought it would and you can't understand why you dreaded doing it so much or put it off for so long.

Media-savvy companies know that reporters who are considering doing a story about the company will check out the company's web site first thing. If the information they need is hard to find or nonexistent, it can make the difference between attracting positive media coverage or not.

Your Web Site Is a Reflection of You and Your Brand

If you don't believe that your web site accurately reflects your company, isn't that saying to a potential customer or journalist, don't believe what you see? You might be correct in saying so, but visitors—and especially reporters—have a hard time discounting what their eyes are telling them. If the latest press release available on your web site is from 1997, it counters your Key Message Point that your company is newsworthy because it is doing new and interesting things.

When it comes to the Internet, the most common mistake business people make is that they think web sites are designed once and that's it. Nothing can be further from the truth. If you want your company to project itself as a newsworthy business, the face you present on the World Wide Web has to be updated regularly to underscore your company's relevance.

Think about it: In 1990, the Internet was populated by tech-savvy cutting-edge consumers. Now, everyone is on it. In 1995, pop-up ads didn't exist. If you designed your web site a few years ago and haven't given it much thought since, then it is clearly time to make sure your web site helps—not hurts—your media outreach efforts.

Another common mistake many executives make is never visiting their own web sites. Before a reporter shows up for your interview, they have been all over your site and they will ask you about the information posted there.

Open your Internet browser and take a critical look at your company's web site. Chances are, it could use a little freshening.

Steps for Making Your Web Site Media Savvy

Before you start redesigning, follow these simple, but media-savvy, principles:

- *Build a press room.* The best way to give reporters the kind of information they want is to create an area just for them. You can call it "Press Room" or "In the News" or "Media Information." Whatever you name the area, make sure that its presence is apparent on your web site's home page and that company contact information is easy to find. Post recent press releases, a company overview, and product lists. Offer reporters an opportunity to register to receive company press releases via e-mail.

- *How does your company look?* If your company is a law firm, the typeface, graphics, and photos you employ on your web site should be different from those on a day care center web site. Make sure that the colors and fonts you use support your communications goals and key message points.

- *Simplicity is best.* Fancy graphics are great, but remember that the more complex the design of your site, the longer it will take to load. Web-surfing reporters don't have time to wait while your graphic or animation loads onto their computer screen.

Keep it simple to keep reporters from clicking over to the next site. If you have to sacrifice flash for speed, so be it.

- *Feed it consistently.* Sure, you want to attract first-time visitors, but it is even more important to keep first-timers coming back for more. Invest in a software program that allows you to add information easily. When your company is featured in a media story, secure the rights and permissions to link to the story. When you issue a press release, make sure it is added to your web site. Add links to related industry sites. Companies with successful web strategies update their content at least once a week. You might not have the time and resources to spend on that level of commitment, but certainly you can do a review every quarter. Create a page that features company executives' essays on current issues and news developments in your industry. Add case studies of client success stories.

- *Emphasize accuracy.* Make sure your web site actually does what it says it will. If you have a "contact us" e-mail option, click on it and make sure an e-mail form appears; you'd be amazed at how many of these links fail.

- *Invent and edit.* Don't merely scan your company brochure into your computer and onto your web site and call it web content. No matter how beautiful your brochure, it doesn't necessarily translate well from paper to electronic media. When you read something on the web, it is a different experience than if you are holding the company brochure in your hand and reading it. For one thing, on the Internet, people tend to scan documents; they don't read everything word for word. Write your Internet documents in a way that helps people scan. Employ bulleted lists and charts because they are easy to read and supply more information in less space.

- *Monitor the news.* The Internet has fundamentally changed the way issues that affect your business emerge and get into the news. With just one computer and a dial-up connection, one person can create a controversy by placing a single posting on a message board or starting a chain-reaction e-mail campaign.

More and more, issues that start on the Internet cross over into traditional media outlets and become national stories. Companies that have been targets of fictional "urban myths"—for instance, the e-mails that announce Bill Gates of Microsoft will send you a dollar for every time you forward this e-mail—know this all too well. Preempt those issues before they get rolling by regularly checking industry web sites for issues that could affect your company. Read message boards in case a disgruntled customer posts an unflattering message about your company. You cannot put out a competing message or set the record straight if you don't know what people are saying about you.

- *Look closely at the message you're sending.* One of my clients, a highly regarded financial consulting firm, designed their web site so that the home page was a beautiful color photo of their empty waiting room. This is a business comprised of senior-level consultants who need to make a personal connection with potential clients! Their furniture photographed well, but the photo contributed nothing to the firm's image or reputation with clients. First impressions last so make sure that yours is one that you want to make stick.

An up-to-date, well-designed web site will not only appeal to your consumers but it might add to your ability to garner media attention. Reporters will look at your web site; make sure it reinforces your Key Message Points and your overall brand message.

KEY POINTS

➤ Web sites need to be updated regularly to provide up-to-date information about your company.

➤ Write your web site's content so that readers can easily scan the information.

➤ Make sure that the look of your site reflects the image you want your company to project.

➤ Stay away from graphics that take too long to load.

> **HOMEWORK**
>
> ➤ Search on the Internet for three web sites of companies that are in your industry. Tour each site thoroughly, making a list of the various information components. Does the web site have an easy-to-find repository of past press releases? Are the press releases recent or are they several years old? Is current public relations contact information posted in a clear manner? Is there any particular feature on someone else's web site that sparks an idea for yours?

PR Lessons from Law School

Lesson Plan

In this final chapter, we learn what lawyers can teach us about communicating with the media. Lawyers can be great communicators, but they are often challenging media training students. This chapter wraps up a number of major points, using the mistakes legal eagles can make as a model for reminding you what not to do when you're in front of the camera.

Of all the clients I have worked with, the most challenging are lawyers. However, throughout my career, there has been no avoiding them.

As a reporter, I covered their cases and sought their expert opinions for my stories. In addition, after the O. J. Simpson murder trial ended, and I decided I wanted to stop reporting and begin the public relations phase of my career, I went to work for a law firm.

My job, as director of communications for Public Counsel Law Center, was to help the attorneys get publicity for their cases.

Getting publicity was relatively easy because the firm was one of the nation's largest pro bono, public interest law firms. Then-Executive Director Steven A. Nissen was a well-known expert on issues that journalists find compelling and want to cover, such as children's rights, immigration policy, and inner-city economic development.

However, the hard part came when the journalists showed up to do the stories, because it quickly became obvious that the attorneys had difficulty in communicating with reporters.

It is easy to understand why many of the lawyers struggled with their interviews. Journalists ask a simple question and look for a simple answer. The attorneys, however, would begin their answer by giving a brief history of the finer legal points on the subject at hand. By the time they got around to answering the question, the reporter's eyes had glazed over and they were looking for a way out.

I started to develop *Media Training 101* in response to the lawyers with whom I worked. Often, attorneys can be resistant to employing *Media Training 101* because it goes against what they have learned in law school and in the courtroom. For example, law students are taught to use all of the proper legal terms. However, this jargon is simply not interesting to a mass audience.

Another reason that training lawyers in media relations can be challenging is that many lawyers started out by wanting to be journalists. Perhaps they shelved that ambition when they found out the average journalism salary, but they haven't lost the desire, and many lawyers not so secretly—yet over-confidently—think they know what makes the media tick. Their legal papers might get high marks from a judge, but that doesn't mean lawyers are superior writers. In fact, the legal writing style often is passive and stilted—not interesting to the general public.

Often, lawyers need media training more than anyone else because they are frequently at the forefront of the news. Many of our top politicians are lawyers. When a sensational crime is committed, it is the lawyer who faces the news media. When there is a civil rights movement afoot, it is the lawyers who lead the quest. When a business goes into bankruptcy, it is the lawyers who speak for the company and explain the bankruptcy to the employees as well as the media.

It's true that many lawyers are natural communicators. Often, lawyers have extensive writing and verbal skills because being a successful lawyer means writing persuasive briefs and successfully stating your arguments.

However, the very qualities that make lawyers competent at the practice of law can sometimes get in their way when they communicate with the media. The following list of the common mistakes lawyers make when dealing with the media offers some valuable lessons for those of us who never went to law school:

Top Lawyer Media Mistakes

- *Talking in legalese:* Regular people do not know what *habeas corpus* and *voir dire* mean, and if they don't know what you mean, they won't understand your message. If you must use a legal term, make sure you immediately define it for the reporter and/or your audience. High-tech experts face the same challenge when they use computer speak that the rest of us find confusing and intimidating.

- *Never using your firm's name:* Let's say a CEO watches a lawyer being interviewed and is so impressed, he wants to hire the lawyer's firm. How will the CEO know how to get in touch with the lawyer if the lawyer never states the name of her firm? The rest of us need to remember that when interviewed about our company, we don't want the audience to think the name of our company is "we" or "us."

- *Failing to recognize that winning in the court of law and losing in the court of public opinion is not a victory:* The best lawyers know this rule well; if you don't believe me, just take a look at O. J. Simpson. Nonlawyers often are stunned that their companies can be proven to be innocent but can still be tarnished by a scandal.

- *Answering only the question:* An interview is not testimony. Yes and No answers are required in a courtroom, but outside, in the real business world, Yes and No alone don't cut it. When you answer a reporter's question, remember to employ the ABC *formula:* Answer the question; Bridge to a Key Message Point; Conclude by telling your audience what to make of the facts.

- *Never giving the other side an inch:* If you constantly rage against the other side, people get tired of listening to you and begin turning against you. You gain much more credibility in the court of public opinion if you occasionally give the opposition a little credit. You can say something like, "Well, the other side made this particular point and they are correct. But when I look at additional facts, I draw a different conclusion. That is why I believe my client will triumph in the end . . ." This makes you sound much more reasonable, and as a result, people will listen more closely to what you have to say and give it more weight.

- *Waiting to return a reporter's phone call:* Reporters have deadlines for a reason. Lawyers are often very busy, but if they want to have any relationship with journalists, they need to return reporter's phone calls as soon as possible.

- *Saying "no comment":* As I've noted in earlier chapters, saying "no comment" connotes guilt. Instead, say something like, "The judge has asked us not to comment on the specific pieces of evidence, but what I can say is that when all the evidence is in, I believe my client will be exonerated." Or you might note, "It's too early for me to know the answer to that question, but I can assure you that we are leaving no stone unturned in our quest for the truth."

- *Acting as if reporters are the enemy:* Well, they might be, but that still doesn't mean you have to treat them badly. Be polite; it's for your own good. If a reporter asks you an obnoxious question and you snap, I can assure you that the question isn't going into the news report, but your sarcastic comeback is going to be broadcast far and wide.

- *Taking too long in building up to the primary point:* The public's attention span is short and so is the media's. The average sound bite on a broadcast news report is about five seconds long. If you don't make the most of your time, you will lose your opportunity to put your ideas into the marketplace. Give your facts and make your point quickly.

KEY POINTS

It can be challenging to train lawyers for the media, but their mistakes are useful for anyone learning how to communicate with the press. Avoid the following mistakes common to lawyers:

➤ Define technical terms and industry jargon.

➤ Use your firm's name when you give an interview.

➤ Draw the conclusion for the interviewer and your audience.

➤ Coordinate legal and media strategies.

➤ Acknowledge the other side's arguments and then explain why the other side is wrong.

➤ Promptly return all reporters' phone calls.

➤ Treat reporters with respect and professional friendliness.

➤ Resist the urge to say "no comment."

➤ State your primary point and then back it up with the facts and proof.

HOMEWORK

➤ Make a list of five technical terms or industry jargon that are commonly used in your business. Write short definitions—no more than 10 words per definition—for those terms.

➤ During practice interview sessions, if you use a technical term, make sure that you immediately give the layperson's definition.

CONCLUSION

G raduation season is almost upon us. Just one last piece of business remains: The *Media Training 101* final exam.

If you have done your homework along the way, this exam should be a snap. It's just three questions and you can start any time you like.

Question 1: Name three things you learned about reporters from reading this book.

Question 2: List three *Media Training 101* strategies you have learned to incorporate in your media opportunities.

Question 3: Identify three ways you are going to improve the quality of public relations for your company.

Now that you know the basics of how reporters operate and how to generate positive publicity and give a great interview, you're ready to become a media star!

GLOSSARY

###: The symbol at the end of a company's news release that signifies the end of the release.

A-Head: The feature story in the middle of the front page of *The Wall Street Journal*.

Air Checks: Videotapes that contain a complete story or segment as it actually aired, along with the station's logo and the anchor's introduction to the story.

Associated Press (AP): The nation's largest and highly respected news wire service. Founded in 1848 by six New York City newspaper editors who decided to share the high cost of transmitting news by telegraph, the AP is a nonprofit cooperative, with membership fees paid by news outlets throughout the world. The AP staff reports and distributes news and photos to nearly 1,500 newspapers and 3,900 broadcast outlets in the United States and 15,000 news organizations throughout the world. AP stories are often picked up by other media for wider distribution. Additionally, stories that are aired or published by an AP member organization often are picked up by the AP service and distributed to other member organizations that have the option of running it, too.

Attribution: Naming the person to whom a fact or story is asscribed.

Backgrounder: A document about a company, organization, or event that provides significant history and facts. It is the mainstay of a press kit.

Blast Fax: A press release or media alert that is faxed simultaneously to multiple reporters and newsrooms with the intention of heightening the media's awareness of an upcoming event.

BLT: "Bright, light, and tight." A smoothly written, succinct, often quirky, and usually fun news story.

Boilerplate: The last paragraph in a news release that typically includes a company's location, basic mission statement, and accomplishments. Boilerplates should not change from press release to press release.

Broadsheet: A newspaper that is the same size as *The New York Times.*

B-Roll: Footage shot by news organizations and PR professionals for news packages, promotions, Web casts, and so on. Once the footage is in hand, production companies and PR professionals distribute it to news organizations for their use. B-roll tapes usually feature exterior shots, signage, manufacturing shots, product shots, people walking to or through an office, people shopping or congregating, and people working in an office. Some say the "B" is for background roll, others insist the "B" is for broadcast roll. Over the past few years, some in-house PR departments have begun to produce it and call it business roll.

Budget: A list of stories in the works and under consideration for publication or broadcast. Before your story makes it into a magazine or newspaper, it first has to make it into the budget and that often is a tougher sell.

By-Line: The name of the writer who wrote the article. Usually published below the headline and above the story.

Copy: Text of a story.

Cover Line: A headline on the cover of a magazine.

Credit Line: Small type that credits a photographer with a published photo, usually located under the right side of a photo.

Crossed the Wire: The date and time when a story first appeared on a wire service. Generally, when a company issues a press release, the paid wire service e-mails or telephones a notice that gives the exact time the release "crossed the wire."

Dateline: The text at the start of every published news story that gives the date and city location of the news event the story is about. The popular NBC magazine program took this as its name.

Daybook: Wire services like the Associated Press put out a Daybook every morning that lists the newsworthy events (including addresses, contacts' phone numbers, and technical details for live remotes to newscasts). Many big cities have a local wire service that sends a similar Daybook listing to their member news organizations. If you get your event listed on the Daybook, you are virtually guaranteed coverage.

Deadline: The time that a story must be turned in to editors or executive producers. Deadlines are not negotiable.

Downlink: Recording a satellite feed at the destination.

Drop a Dime: Place a phone call, usually to tell a reporter valuable information that you don't want attributed to yourself.

Dub: A copy of a story on a videocassette, audiocassette, CD, or DVD.

Edit Bay: The room or workstation containing the computers and monitors used for editing a broadcast story.

Embargo: A date on a press release, after which the news becomes public and the generator of the press release gives permission to news outlets to publish the release. Embargoes were more important in the days when organizations depended on the U.S. mail to release news—before e-mail and faxes enabled anyone with a computer to release news instantaneously to every reporter on a media list.

Exclusive: This term has a lot of different meanings, and the meaning employed depends on who's talking. "Exclusive" should connote a story or an interview that no other media outlet has. However, the way the term is often used today could mean only that no other outlet has the interview this week—or even this minute.

Fact Sheet: A document that gives reporters the basic facts about a company or event. A Fact Sheet is usually presented in bullet form, to give reporters essential information at a glance.

Feature: A news story that does not rely on breaking news, but provides colorful details and/or is an interesting read. In print, it is usually accompanied by photos.

Feed: Transmitting a story or interview via satellite or fiber for distribution to media outlets. For example, every afternoon, CBS *Evening News* feeds their broadcast to CBS stations and affiliates.

Five Ws and the H: Who, What, Where, When, Why, and How are the six essential elements of any piece of journalism and the first thing any journalist learns. In the early days of mass media, a lead had to contain each of the five Ws and the H.

Flack: Slang for a public relations professional, customarily used in a derogatory manner. However, when public relations professionals use it themselves, the effect often disarms skeptical reporters and breaks the ice.

Get: Snagging an exclusive interview with a prominent news subject. For example, Barbara Walters scored the Get for landing the interview with Senator Hillary Clinton about her book *Living History* and Katie Couric landed a big Get by convincing the family of murder victim Laci Peterson to grant her their first big interview.

Gofer: They go for coffee, go pick up lunch, go drive the tape back to the station. A good gofer is worth his or her weight in gold.

Government in the Sunshine: A series of Florida laws that mandate unfettered public access to official meetings and documents.

Green Room: The room you wait in before it's your turn to go into a news studio for an interview. Green Rooms are usually furnished with a coffee pot, a water cooler, a mirror, and a couple of beat-up couches. The bigger the show, the better the Green Room is.

Grip: Professional in the TV studio in charge of lighting.

Groomer: A makeup artist.

Hack: Slang for a lifetime news media professional. Not usually meant as a compliment.

Head Shot: A photo of a news subject's face.

Hit: A story that is published or aired.

IFB: The little earpiece that a guest/commentator wears during a live remote TV interview. The IFB comes with a volume dial. Always turn up the volume a little louder than you think you will need it, because although during the sound check, you hear everything clearly the minute the interview begins, it always seems that the sound grows fainter.

Indirect Quote: In a story, reporting the gist of what someone said, without employing the exact words used.

Lavaliere Mike: The small microphone that is clipped on to an interviewee's shirt or jacket. Be careful to never touch the mike when gesturing with your hands or you get a loud static-filled sound.

Lead: The first sentence or paragraph of a story that reveals the relevant news developments. The lead sets the tone for the story. In the old days, leads had to contain the five Ws and the H, but these days, just one will do.

Live Mike: A microphone that is on and transmitting sound. Treat every mike you see as live.

Live Shot: An interview or news story that is transmitted live from the location of a news event.

Lock-Up: A phrase generally used by TV producers to signify that they have an exclusive interview. For example, *60 Minutes* locked up Duke University officials for a story about the lethal mistakes during a transplant that cost a teenager her life.

Long-Leads: Usually a weekly, monthly, or quarterly publication that has deadlines weeks, or even months, before the publication hits the newsstands. Occasionally used to describe TV programs like *Frontline* or *60 Minutes* that devote substantial amounts of time researching stories. As technology keeps speeding up, and as media competition grows ever more intense, the long leads grow shorter and shorter.

Media Alert: A head's up notice that is e-mailed to reporters, producers, and news assignment desks giving the five Ws of an upcoming news event.

Mediagenic: Interview subjects who look and sound good in press conferences and during TV interviews. The camera loves them; reporters and producers love them even more—at least for a while.

Media Hog: A well-known, quotable person who offers himself for interviews on multiple news events. When a new media hog appears on the scene of a news story, reporters and producers are grateful to have someone quotable and knowledgeable at their disposal. However, overexposure can lead to reporters sniping that "he'd go to the opening of an envelope."

Mug Shot: A photo of a news subject's face or "mug." A slang term for **Head Shot.**

News Conference (or Press Conference): To be used with discretion and only for announcements of primary significance. Reporters seldom have time to attend press conferences unless the president is fielding questions, a major company is responding to a significant company event or governemtn crisis, or an A-list celebrity is involved. Press conferences are most useful to participants and the press when dozens of media outlets are covering the same story. For example, police departments hold press conferences to announce developments in a notorious crime. As we all saw during the Iraq War, various departments of the federal government hold press conferences to announce news of universal interest.

News Peg: The reason why the story is relevant now and why it is in the news today. For example, the fortieth anniversary of President John F. Kennedy's assassination is the news peg for a host of stories about the illustrious clan. Also called a *news hook*.

No Comment: The single worst thing you could possibly say to a reporter or when in front of a video camera.

Not for Attribution: A piece of information that you should be very careful with and tell only to a reporter that you can trust completely.

Off-the-Record: Something you are never going to say to a news reporter.

On Background: Giving an interview or a portion of the interview when the reporter understands that anything you say is just for background information and not for direct attribution. Also known as playing with dynamite since you have no control over what the reporter chooses to do with the background.

On Demand: Archived information and images that are stored on a server and, for a fee, can be accessed via the Internet on demand.

On-the-Record: Everything you ever say to a news reporter. Even if it never makes print or air, reporters, who love to gossip, will probably tell somebody.

Op-Ed: An opinion column that is published on the page opposite the editorial page.

Paraphrase: When a reporter reports what you said, without using direct quotes.

Pay-to-Play: Also called *advertorials,* these are essentially print or broadcast media for which a company pays. Often, these programs have names that are strikingly similar to real news outlets and their pitch to companies includes the fact that major entities are participating. However, often those companies are receiving the opportunity for free; their participation is a strong lure to smaller companies.

Photo Caption: The text that accompanies a published photograph.

Pickup: A story that is retransmitted. For example, a press release can be picked up by a **Wire Service** or a **Video News Release** can be picked up by a local TV newscast.

Pitch: When a **Flack** contacts a reporter to try to interest him or her in doing a particular story. If the reporter is interested, then he, in turn, has to pitch the story idea to his editors. When pitching a reporter, always provide enough facts to answer the editors' tough questions.

Pitch Memo: A memo, usually e-mailed and never lengthier than one computer screen, that lays out the story idea and provides factual background information.

Post Production: The phase during which the actual segment for a news show is edited. Editing is the single most important phase of putting together a story.

Press Kit: A folder that contains information about a company, event, or organization. The best press kits are simple. Many companies make their press kits available on their web sites.

Producer: The person in charge of all logistics involved in executing a story or interview for radio, TV, or **Web Cast.** For a single story, there might be a field producer, who is on the scene of the news, as well as a producer in the newsroom, who supervises the overall news gathering. The reporter may be the face on the newscast, but the producer often holds more power over the way the story is told.

Proof: Short for proofreading—a dying art.

Public Service Announcement (PSA): A 15- or 30-second commercial for a charitable organization. Radio and TV outlets air PSAs free of charge for the purpose of informing the public.

Puff Piece: A feature story that paints the main character in a most flattering light.

Pull-Quote: A quote contained within a story that is pulled out and enlarged.

Radio Media Tour (RMT): A series of radio interviews conducted over the phone between a spokesperson and an anchor or a deejay. Generally, the spokesperson is scheduled for phone interviews in a variety of markets, one right after the other. The interviews can be either live or taped.

Raw Footage: Tape as it was shot and before it goes through editing.

Roundup: A story that rounds up a variety of developments in a broad, ongoing story.

Satellite Media Tour (SMT): A series of TV interviews conducted from one studio or remote location. As the interview subject sits in a studio, he or she does a different interview, in a different market, every few minutes. The interviews can be either live or taped.

Second-Day Story: A news story published or aired on the day after the news first breaks. A second-day story usually puts the event into a wider context.

Shoot: Bringing together a producer, audio technician, and a camera operator to shoot footage of a news story.

Sidebar: A shorter story, usually employing a feature or quirky angle, that is published adjacent to a straight news story.

Slates: Text on a plain background that gives information about the footage that follows.

Sound on Tape (SOT): Recorded sounds or sound bites.

Subhead: The secondary title of a news release.

Tabloid: Today, tabloid can be an adjective to describe a gossip-mongering, careless, and sensationalizing press corps, but it started out meaning a newspaper whose pages were half the size of *The New York Times.*

Talking Head: An interview subject. Often used in the context of a producer worrying that there are "too many talking heads" and not enough action shots during a story.

Video News Release (VNR): A company-produced news feature. Companies then transmit their VNRs to news stations that might include it in their newscasts. VNRs that are overly commercial-like usually don't get much pick-up.

Walk-and-Talk: Footage contained in many TV news stories in which the interviewer and the interviewee are walking outside while conducting the interview. Barbara Walters is famous for these.

Web Cast: A live or on-demand broadcast or meeting that can be watched online.

Wire Service: A news-gathering company or cooperative, such as Associated Press, Bloomberg News, United Press International, and Reuters. For a fee, usually based on circulation or audience size, wire services provide other news organizations with news stories.

White Paper: A technical paper published in a professional journal. Often technical companies offer prospective customers free copies of their White Papers.

ACKNOWLEDGMENTS

Just a few weeks ago, I was at a party for a client, Jennifer Kushell, who was celebrating the publication of her *New York Times* best-seller, *Secrets of the Young & Successful: How to Get Everything You Want Without Waiting a Lifetime* (Simon and Schuster, 2003). A television news reporter circulated among the crowd, asking attendees to tell their own career success stories.

When the reporter reached my table, he asked, "What have you achieved that your friends and family never thought you could?"

Knowing that *Media Training 101* was about to be published, my friend from my college newspaper, Michael Szymanski, now the managing editor of Zap2it.com, turned to me and asked if achieving my lifelong dream of publishing a book surprised my friends and family.

"No," I said. "My friends and family always thought I could do anything I wanted to do. The only person I ever surprised was me."

That simple reality means that I have many people to thank for their guidance, true friendship, and support. Without them, *Media Training 101* might have remained a dream.

At John Wiley & Sons, Airié Stuart, my editor; Jessica Noyes, assistant editor; Emily Conway, editorial assistant; Linda Witzling, production manager; and Nancy Land, head of the production team at Publications Development Company of Texas, have been my own personal Dream Team.

My literary agent, Joelle Delbourgo, used her 20 years of experience in the publishing world to guide me through the long process of writing and development. Thank you, Joelle, for starting and sustaining me on this journey.

I am privileged to belong to a large family of writers, artists, doctors, and business leaders who inspire me. Thanks and love to Audrey and Nathan Koss, Joan and Harvey Friedman, Norman and Ruth Block, Allison Sullivan and Robin Friedman. Special hugs go to my six siblings, Michael Stewart, Martha Sharp, Barbara Wangrin, David Stewart, Robin Stewart, and Cathy Fingerman, because all that fighting we did as kids prepared me to become a passionate advocate for my clients! Love and thanks also go to my brothers- and sister-in-law: Mark Wangrin, Mark Sharp, Irwin Fingerman, Lori Stewart, and Jeff Sullivan. Our family's new generation challenges me to keep up with them, so thanks to Matthew and Michael Finkelstein; Shera, Levi, and Seth Fingerman; Haley Sharp; Chad, Chloe, and Carly Stewart; Makala and Ben Wangrin; Hannah and Abigail Sullivan; and Jordan and Lily Rowe.

Also, a special note of thanks to my late father, Bernie Stewart, whose career in advertising meant that our family's dinner table conversations were dissections of current events and media campaigns. Dad, I owe you a milkshake.

Throughout my career, I have been fortunate to know and work with many who encouraged me, usually by their own example, and pushed me forward when my own legs wouldn't budge: Lynn Basmajian, Doug Bennett, Bill Boyarsky, Eli Broad, Lou Cannon; Mary Cannon; Allen Carrier, Margaret Carroll, Michelle Caruso, John Combs, Marsha "Cookie" Cooke, Jerry Della Femina, Morris Dees, Kim Dozier, Bob Dubill, Dominick Dunne, Gwen Flanders, Michael Greenberg, Amy Goldsmith, Jody Henenfeld, Dan Katzir, Dennis Kneale, Michelle Koch, Dan Laikin, Laurie Levenson, Jayne Lytell, Nora Manella, Alice McQuillan, Doug Mirell, Scooter Naney, Steve Nissen, Jennifer Openshaw, Rick Orlov, Scott Painter, Phil Paccione, Tom Poletti, Bill Rosendahl, Jeff Rowe, Diane Sodetz, Susan Spillman, Gretchen Struble, Lisa Weil, Henry Weinstein, Shlomit Weisblum, Elisa Wiefel, Cliff Young, and every single member of the press corps of the O. J. Simpson murder trial.

Special thanks to my former colleagues at at USA Today, Public Counsel Law Center, Sitrick and Company, Edelman Public Relations Worldwide, and APCO Worldwide.

Even news junkies need to re-charge their batteries every once in a while, so special thanks go to Monica Taylor and all "the girls" of Needlepoint on Montana; the caretakers of Palisade Park; and Ira Rosen, Jane Alpert, and everyone at Power Yoga of Santa Monica.

My final thank you is reserved for someone truly unforgetable. I began my career at The Independent Florida Alligator, the nation's first independent college daily, and that experience not only enriched my life but also gave my career its focus. For generations of Alligator alumni, Ed Barber, the general manager as well as the lone official grown-up at the Alligator office, has made sure that University of Florida students had their own newsroom in which they could turn their ideas into words and their words into stories. Thank you, Mr. Barber, for giving all of us a place to learn that if we are willing, dreams can come to life.

INDEX

ABOUT THE AUTHOR

Sally Stewart is a former journalist who worked for *USA Today* for 13 years, covering some of the biggest stories of the day, including the O. J. Simpson murder trial, the Los Angeles riots, and the Rodney King beating trials. Throughout her journalism career, which began at *The Independent Florida Alligator* at the University of Florida, she appeared frequently on CNN and other television and radio current affairs programs. Since 1996, she has worked as a communications consultant for a variety of public companies, private enterprises, and nonprofit organizations. Today, she heads her own consulting group, SA Stewart Communications, headquartered in Santa Monica, California. She also is a member of the Board of Creative Advisors of *National Lampoon*. Visit her web site at www.mediatraining101.com.